PHOTOGRAPHIS 87

The International Annual of Photography

Das internationale Jahrbuch der Photographie

Le répertoire international de la photographie

Edited by/Herausgegeben von/Réalisé par

B. Martin Pedersen

Editor and Art Director: B. Martin Pedersen
Assistant Editor: Joan Lüssi
Project Managers: Romy Herzog, Heinke Jenssen
Designers: Marino Bianchera, Martin Byland
Art Assistant: Walter Zuber

Graphis Press Corp., Zurich (Switzerland)

Graphis U.S. Inc., New York, N.Y. (USA)

GRAPHIS PUBLICATIONS

GRAPHIS, International bi-monthly journal of graphic art and applied art
GRAPHIS ANNUAL, The international annual on design and illustration
PHOTOGRAPHIS, The international annual on photography
GRAPHIS POSTERS, The international annual of poster art
GRAPHIS PACKAGING VOL. 4, An international survey of package design
CHILDREN'S BOOK ILLUSTRATION VOL. 4, An international survey of children's book illustration
GRAPHIS DIAGRAMS, The graphic visualization of abstract data
FILM + TV GRAPHICS 2, An international survey of the art of film animation
ARCHIGRAPHIA, Architectural and environmental graphics
GRAPHIS EPHEMERA, Artists' Self-Promotion

GRAPHIS-PUBLIKATIONEN

GRAPHIS, Die internationale Zweimonatszeitschrift für Graphik und angewandte Kunst
GRAPHIS ANNUAL, Das internationale Jahrbuch über Design und Illustration
PHOTOGRAPHIS, Das internationale Jahrbuch der Photographie
GRAPHIS POSTERS, Das internationale Jahrbuch der Plakatkunst
GRAPHIS PACKUNGEN BAND 4, Internationales Handbuch der Packungsgestaltung
KINDERBUCH-ILLUSTRATION BAND 4, Eine internationale Übersicht über die Kinderbuch-Illustration
GRAPHIS DIAGRAMS, Die graphische Visualisierung abstrakter Gegebenheiten
FILM + TV GRAPHICS 2, Ein internationaler Überblick über die Kunst des Animationsfilms
ARCHIGRAPHIA, Architektur- und Umweltgraphik
GRAPHIS EPHEMERA, Künstler-Eigenwerbung

PUBLICATIONS GRAPHIS

GRAPHIS, La revue bimestrielle internationale d'arts graphiques et d'arts appliqués
GRAPHIS ANNUAL, Le répertoire international de la communication visuelle
PHOTOGRAPHIS, Le répertoire international de la photographie
GRAPHIS POSTERS, Le répertoire international de l'art de l'affiche
GRAPHIS EMBALLAGES VOL. 4, Répertoire international des formes de l'emballage
ILLUSTRATIONS DE LIVRES D'ENFANTS VOL. 4, Un aperçu international des illustrations de livres d'enfants
GRAPHIS DIAGRAMS, La visualisation graphique de données abstraites
FILM + TV GRAPHICS 2, Un panorama international de l'art du film d'animation
ARCHIGRAPHIA, La création graphique appliquée à l'architecture et à l'environnement
GRAPHIS EPHEMERA, Autopromotion des artistes

PUBLICATION No. 185 (ISBN 3-85709-287-4)
© Copyright under Universal Copyright Convention
Copyright 1987 by Graphis Press Corp., 107 Dufourstrasse, 8008 Zurich, Switzerland/
Graphis U.S. Inc., 141 Lexington Avenue, New York, N.Y. 10016, USA
No part of this book may be reproduced in any form without written permission of the publisher
Printed in Japan by Dai Nippon
Typeset in Switzerland by Setzerei Heller, Zurich
Typefaces: Garamond ITC Light Condensed, Futura Extra Bold

ABBREVIATIONS

Australia	AUS
Austria	AUT
Belgium	BEL
Canada	CAN
China (People's Republic)	PRC
Costa Rica	CRI
Denmark	DEN
France	FRA
Germany (West)	GER
Great Britain	GBR
Greece	GRE
Hong Kong	HKG
Italy	ITA
Japan	JPN
Netherlands	NLD
Norway	NOR
Spain	SPA
Sweden	SWE
Switzerland	SWI
USA	USA

ABKÜRZUNGEN

Australien	AUS
Belgien	BEL
China (Volksrepublik)	PRC
Costa Rica	CRI
Dänemark	DEN
Deutschland (BRD)	GER
Frankreich	FRA
Griechenland	GRE
Grossbritannien	GBR
Hongkong	HKG
Italien	ITA
Japan	JPN
Kanada	CAN
Niederlande	NLD
Norwegen	NOR
Österreich	AUT
Schweden	SWE
Schweiz	SWI
Spanien	SPA
USA	USA

ABRÉVIATIONS

Allemagne occidentale	GER
Australie	AUS
Autriche	AUT
Belgique	BEL
Canada	CAN
Chine (République populaire)	PRC
Costa Rica	CRI
Danemark	DEN
Espagne	SPA
Etats-Unis	USA
France	FRA
Grande-Bretagne	GBR
Grèce	GRE
Hongkong	HKG
Italie	ITA
Japon	JPN
Norvège	NOR
Pays-Bas	NLD
Suède	SWE
Suisse	SWI

REMARKS

■ Our sincere thanks are extended to all photographers and to everyone who contributed – direct or indirect – to this international annual of photography.

■ Entry instructions may be requested at: Graphis Press Corp., Dufourstrasse 107, 8008 Zurich, Switzerland

ANMERKUNGEN

■ Unser herzlicher Dank gilt allen Photographen und Einsendern, die direkt oder indirekt zu diesem internationalen Jahrbuch der Photographie beigetragen haben.

■ Teilnahmebedingungen: Graphis Verlag AG, Dufourstrasse 107, 8008 Zurich, Schweiz

AVERTISSEMENT

■ Nos sincères remerciements vont à tous les photographes et colloborateurs qui ont apporté leur contribution directe ou indirecte au présent annuel international de la photographie.

■ Demande de participation: Editions Graphis SA, Dufourstrasse 107, 8008 Zurich, Suisse

DR. WILLY ROTZLER

The traditional distinction between fine and commercial photography is no longer justified. If we count out the real amateur, every photo, as soon as it is published, is a kind of commercial photograph, though it may fill that role in several different ways. This holds true for photography executed on assignment for magazines: press and fashion photos, interior shots, as well as those planned down to the last detail that appear in ads, posters and printed matter.

It would seem that the differences lie in the various approaches of the photographers to the individual tasks, whether these tasks are self initiated or commissioned. A photographer who has to capture the way of life of Indios in the Amazon on assignment or for a photo essay, will of necessity take a different line of approach from one who is highlighting the haute couture of the coming season for a fashion house in Rome. The difference in motif, character and style of the shots evolves from the great variety and scope of the tasks undertaken. It stems also from the criteria that other photographers, working on related commissions, have already set. To distinguish oneself as much as possible from the conventional, to be new and different, is without doubt a decisive motivation for individuality in photography.

Every photographer attempts, naturally, to put as much as possible of his or

> A MAJOR INCENTIVE IN CREATING A NEW PHOTOGRAPH IS THE WISH TO DO SOMETHING NEW.

her own personality, pictorial concept, artistic and technical style into their photographs. The viewers will therefore not be asking themselves only as to what extent the photo in question fulfils its purpose. In fact, this may not be their chief concern at all. One might well be more impressed by a photo simply because the photographer has managed to both fulfil the assignment as well as make a personal statement. In other words, a commercial photograph

can still be the expression of a personality, the reflection of a personal style and a particular way of seeing.

If it is considered that photography has, in the course of its eventful history, greatly extended our knowledge of reality and opened up realms of vision that were previously esoteric and inaccessible, anyone who looks at new and unfamiliar photos is justified in asking: "What is new for me in this shot and in what way is it different?" The truth is that every photograph of value, regardless of its intent and purpose, assists in widening and opening up our visual alertness. What the photographer has seen affects our own vision of things. A photo for a perfume ad may be a means to new knowledge just as much as a fashion shot or a photo of a holiday scene. A fast-action sports shot may be just as rewarding as a long and ingeniously set up architectural photo, a still life or a nude.

The black-and-white and color photographs from many countries reproduced on the following pages are the work of numerous photographers, some of them famous, some of them virtually unknown. The complete collection is arranged in sections that place each photo in its specific context. This principle of classification underpins the various approaches taken to tackle similar problems. As a result the photos represent all kinds of moods. They are factual, imaginative, stylized, nonchalant, severe, playful, static, dynamic, cool, committed, hard, tender, serious or lighthearted. Some are technically simple. They do not rely on tricks, but they make subtle use of today's wide choice of lenses and the chemical and physical technologies of the photographic industry.

The principal differences lie in the attitude of the photographer towards the image he wishes to produce. In some photos the photographer is more interested in the message and its expression than in technical quality. In others we see that a perfectionist has been intent on creating a technically flawless visual image. Styles differ widely too; from the ingenious controlled cropping of the subject to fit a preconceived idea (often first tried out with a Polaroid shot) to the moment of truth that is instinctively composed with brilliance, though it may happen by chance. Who would dare to be the judge of so many varied approaches?

The photographic aesthetic also includes that which is not in the picture. That which has been deliberately excluded or suppressed; the mannequin posing in the mysterious emptiness of space as against the model placed in a densely packed atmosphere embodying all the thousand aspects of daily life. Formally designed or even consciously staged photos are in opposition to the seemingly natural - though it is an open question whether the natural is less staged than the formally designed. The photographer's

> EVERY PHOTOGRAPH OF ANY VALUE HELPS TO WIDEN OR DEEPEN OUR IMAGE OF REALITY.

eye may concentrate on a certain motif or element. On the other hand it may wander in the epic sweep of the portrayal.

In contemplating photographs, whether they are spread out across a photographer's or art director's table, or have already been selected for a promotion campaign or a magazine feature, the viewer has to choose between two diametrically opposed procedures. He can simply opt for whatever appeals to his

temperament and taste, or he can play the voyeur, as it were, looking for whatever is unusual, strange or seductive. The photographs collected in this annual will satisfy both: the curiosity for the conventional and accustomed - as well as for the exotic and unfamiliar.

Susan Sontag stated perceptively in her book *On Photography* in 1977, that where photography is able to free our traditional way of seeing from its old habits, it creates a new kind of vision: at once intense and cool, committed yet distanced, enchanted by insignificant detail, fascinated by discord. But photographic vision must be incessantly renewed by thematic or technical shocks in order to convey the impression of a breakaway from ordinary seeing, since our vision has a tendency, when challenged by the revelations of photographers, to adjust to the photographs.

Maybe this is precisely the reason for our insatiable desire to absorb ever new photographic images. The photos contained in this volume will at least give us ample opportunity to satisfy that appetite for a while.

WILLY ROTZLER was born in Basle in 1917 and graduated in art history from the university of his native city. For many years (1948-61) he was curator of the Museum of Applied Arts (Kunstgewerbemuseum) Zurich. From 1962-68 he was editor of the art magazine Du *and since then he has been engaged free-lance in writing and publishing works on art. Among the many books which he has published are studies on Johannes Itten, Camille Graeser, Friedrich Vordemberge-Gildewart, Arturo Bonfanti, Alberto Giacometti as well as "Art and Graphics", "Political and Social Posters in Switzerland", "Heinz Jost, Theater Posters". Numerous essays appear in the magazines* Du *and* Graphis.

DR. WILLY ROTZLER

D ie traditionelle Scheidung von freier und angewandter Photographie hat längst ihren Sinn und ihre Berechtigung verloren. Sieht man vom Tun der reinen Amateure ab, so ist jede Photographie, sobald sie öffentlich wird, in irgendeiner, allerdings unterschiedlichen Weise eine angewandte Photographie. Das gilt für Aufnahmen, die «on assignment» für Zeitschriften gemacht werden, gilt für Presse- oder Modebilder und Interieur-Aufnahmen ebenso wie für motivisch und formal genau kalkulierte Photographien, wie sie bei Inseraten, Plakaten oder Werbedrucksachen Verwendung finden.

Die Unterschiede liegen, so scheint es, im unterschiedlichen Angehen der selbst- oder fremdgestellten Aufgaben. Wer das Leben der Indianer am Amazonas in einer Reportage oder einem Photo-Essay einfängt, geht naturgemäss anders vor als der Photograph, der für ein Modehaus in Rom die «alta moda» der kommenden Saison überhöht einzufangen hat. Die Unterschiede im Motiv, im Charakter und Stil der Aufnahmen ergeben sich zunächst aus der Verschiedenheit der Aufgabenbereiche. Sie ergeben sich aber auch aus den Massstäben, die von anderen Photographen für verwandte Aufgaben bereits gesetzt worden sind. Sich von allem Bestehenden möglichst zu unterscheiden, neu und andersartig zu sein, das ist zweifellos ein entscheidender Antrieb für eigenständige photographische Bilder.

> JEDE PHOTOGRAPHIE
> TRÄGT DAZU BEI, UNSER BILD
> VON DER WIRKLICHKEIT
> ZU ERWEITERN.

Schliesslich versucht jeder Photograph in jede seiner Aufnahmen so viel wie möglich von seiner Persönlichkeit, seinen Bildauffassungen und seinen Stilmitteln im künstlerischen wie im technischen Sinn einzubringen. Stets wird daher der Betrachter von Photographien nicht nur und oft nicht einmal in erster Linie darauf achten, wie weit die gestellte Aufgabe von der in Frage stehenden Aufnahme erfüllt wird. Er wird vielmehr dem Photographen auf die Finger sehen und vom Bild in dem Mass gefangen sein, in dem der Gestalter mit der Kamera seine Sache, also letztlich sich selbst zum Ausdruck gebracht hat. Anders gesagt: Auch eine sogenannt angewandte Photographie ist Ausdruck einer Persönlichkeit, ist Niederschlag einer persönlichen Sehweise, eines persönlichen Stilwillens.

Geht man davon aus, dass die Photographie im Verlauf ihrer bewegten Geschichte unser Wissen über die Wirk-lichkeit entscheidend erweitern konnte, dass sie Bezirke eröffnet hat, die vorher verschlossen und verborgen waren, so darf der Betrachter neuer, ihm bisher nicht bekannter Photographien die Frage stellen: Was zeigt mir diese Aufnahme neu, und was zeigt sie mir anders? Damit trägt jede Photographie von Rang – ungeachtet ihres konkreten Verwendungszweckes – dazu bei, unser Bild von der Wirklichkeit zu erweitern oder zu vertiefen. Durch das, was der Photograph gesehen hat, wird auch unsere Sicht auf die Dinge erweitert und verändert. Zu einem solchen Erkenntnismittel kann die Photographie für eine Parfüm-Anzeige ebenso werden wie eine Mode-Aufnahme oder das Bild einer Ferienlandschaft. Erkenntnismittel kann eine blitzschnelle Sportaufnahme ebenso sein wie eine ausgeklügelte Architektur-Photographie, ein Stilleben oder ein Frauenbein.

Die auf den folgenden Seiten versammelten schwarzweissen und farbigen Photographien aus vielen Ländern zeigen Arbeiten einer grossen Zahl von teils bekannten, teils noch unbekannten Photographen. Die Auswahl ist in einige Kapitel gegliedert, die das einzelne Bild zumindest grob in den ihm zugehörenden Rahmen stellen. Gerade ein solch äusserliches Ordnungsprinzip macht sichtbar, wie unterschiedlich die einzelnen Photographen ihre Aufgabe angehen und zu lösen suchen. So strahlen diese Aufnahmen eine Vielzahl von «Stimmungen» aus; sie sind sachlich oder phantasievoll, hoch-stilisiert oder lässig, streng oder verspielt, statisch oder dynamisch, distanziert kühl oder leidenschaftlich engagiert, hart oder weich, ernst oder heiter. Sie sind tech-nisch einfach, ohne Aufnahme- und Labor-Tricks, oder aber sie nutzen raffi-niert alle Möglichkeiten der hochentwik-kelten Kamera, der Objektivwahl und der Zauberei in Dunkelkammer und Labor.

Unterschiede aber gibt es vor allem im Verhalten des Photographen dem von ihm zu schaffenden Bild gegenüber. Da gibt es die Aufnahme, bei der es dem Pho-tographen mehr um die Aussage, um den Ausdruck geht als um technische Quali-tät. Und da gibt es die technisch makellose Arbeit der Perfektionisten. Aber auch die eigentlichen Stilmittel sind denkbar ver-schieden: Der formal ausgeklügelte Aus-schnitt des Bildes als Resultat eines vor-bedachten Konzepts (manchmal schnell mit einem Polaroid erprobt) steht der instinktiven, manchmal sogar dem Zufall Raum gebenden Bildgestalt gegenüber. Wer wagte da, Noten auszuteilen?

Zur photographischen Ästhetik gehört aber auch das, was im Bild nicht erscheint, was willentlich weggelassen oder ausgeschaltet, ausgemerzt wurde: das in die geheimnisvolle Leere des Rau-mes gestellte Mannequin gegenüber dem in eine dichte, vom Tausenderlei des Tages geprägte Atmosphäre eingebette-ten Modell ... Formal betonte oder gar formalistisch zurechtgemachte Bilder

ERKENNTNISMITTEL KANN EINE BLITZSCHNELLE SPORTAUFNAHME EBENSO SEIN WIE EIN STILLEBEN.

stehen den scheinbar ganz natürlichen gegenüber, wobei durchaus offenbleibt, ob Natürlichkeit weniger inszeniert ist als bewusste Stilisierung. Der Blick des Pho-tographen kann sich auf ein bestimmtes Motiv oder Element konzentrieren, er kann umgekehrt aber auch schweifend sein, im epischen Schildern sich verlieren.

Beim Betrachten von Photographien, seien sie auf dem Ateliertisch des Photo-graphen oder des Bildredaktors aufgelegt oder seien sie bereits selektionierter Bestandteil einer Werbeaktion oder eines Zeitschriften-Beitrags, sieht sich der Betrachter hin- und hergerissen zwi-schen zwei gegensätzlichen Haltungen: Soll er sich bekennen zu dem, was ihm temperamentmässig und geschmacklich entspricht und entgegenkommt, oder soll er sich lustvoll, in einer beinahe voyeuri-stischen Haltung, einsehen in das Fremde, Andersartige, somit Verführe-rische? Die hier versammelten Photogra-phien sprechen beides an: die Neugier auf

das Gewohnte und Vertraute und die Neugier auf das exotisch Fremdartige, Verrückte und zum Seh-Abenteuer Ver-lockende.

Die gescheite Susan Sontag sagt in ihren Betrachtungen «Über Photogra-phie» (On Photography, 1977): «Sofern die Photographie das herkömmliche Sehen tatsächlich von seinen Verkrustun-gen befreit, schafft sie eine neue Art des Sehens: intensiv und zugleich kühl, enga-giert und zugleich distanziert, verzaubert vom unbedeutenden Detail, fasziniert von der Disharmonie. Aber das photogra-phische Sehen muss unentwegt durch neue thematische oder technische Schocks erneuert werden, um den Ein-druck des Bruchs mit dem gewöhnlichen Sehen zu vermitteln. Denn herausgefor-dert durch die Offenbarungen der Photo-graphen, hat das Sehen die Tendenz, sich den Photographien anzupassen.»

Es mag sein, dass gerade darin der Grund für unser unersättliches Bedürfnis liegt, uns mit Heisshunger auf immer neue photographische Bilder zu stürzen. Die in diesem Band vereinten Aufnahmen sind eine gute Wegzehrung.

WILLY ROTZLER, 1917 in Basel geboren, promovierte in Kunstgeschichte an der dortigen Universität. Von 1948-61 arbeitete er als Konservator am Kunstgewerbemu-seum Zürich. In den Jahren 1962-68 war er Redaktor der Kunstzeitschrift Du, *seither arbeitet er als freier Kunst-publizist. Zu den zahlreichen Büchern, die er veröffent-lichte, gehören Monographien über Johannes Itten, Camille Graeser, Friedrich Vordemberge-Gildewart, Arturo Bonfanti, Alberto Giacometti sowie die Bücher* Kunst und Graphik, Politische und soziale Plakate in der Schweiz, Heinz Jost, Theaterplakate. *Zahlreiche Aufsätze erschienen in den Zeitschriften* Du *und* Graphis.

DR WILLY ROTZLER

Il y a longtemps que la distinction traditionnelle entre création photographique libre et photographie appliquée a perdu son sens et sa raison d'être. Abstraction faite des clichés d'amateurs, toute photo rendue publique est d'une manière ou d'une autre une photo appliquée, même si les différences de l'une à l'autre sont notables. Il en est ainsi des photos de commande pour les magazines, des photos de presse ou de mode, des photos d'intérieur, mais aussi des photos construites d'après un motif ou un plan formel précis pour une annonce, une affiche, un imprimé.

Les différences d'une photo à l'autre résultent, semble-t-il, de l'approche, de la manière dont est abordée une tâche imposée ou choisie délibérément. On procédera autrement pour enregistrer la vie des Indiens d'Amazonie dans un reportage ou un essai photo que pour la mise en pages d'une collection de la haute couture romaine, c'est là l'évidence même. Les différences de motif, de caractère, de style sont dues en première analyse à la diversité des domaines de la création photographique. Elles résultent toutefois aussi des standards déjà adoptés par d'autres photographes pour des travaux similaires. Se distinguer autant que possible du tout-venant, être novateur, différent, voilà l'une des motivations-clefs pour la réalisation photographique d'envergure.

En fin de compte, chaque photographe tente d'incorporer dans chacune

> ## SE DISTINGUER DU TOUT-VENANT, VOILÀ L'UNE DES CLEFS DE LA PHOTOGRAPHIE.

de ses photos autant d'éléments que possible de sa personnalité, de sa conception de l'image, de ses moyens stylistiques au plan artistique et technique. C'est ce qui fait qu'en regardant une photo, on ne prêtera pas seulement (et souvent pas d'emblée) attention à la manière dont la tâche imposée a été remplie. On s'attachera plutôt à la démarche du photographe, et la photo sera d'autant plus accrochante que son réalisateur aura mieux traduit dans le langage visuel le regard qu'il porte en lui. Ce qui revient à dire que même la photographie dite appliquée est l'expression d'une personnalité, le précipité d'une vision personnelle, d'une volonté stylistique personnelle.

En reconnaissant qu'au cours de son histoire mouvementée, la photographie a sensiblement élargi notre perception du

réel en nous donnant accès à des domaines inconnus ou cachés, on sera amené à poser au sujet de chaque nouvelle photo la question suivante: Est-ce que cette photo me montre quelque chose de nouveau, et autrement? Toute photo d'importance contribue ainsi à élargir notre vision du réel ou à l'approfondir, quel que soit l'usage concret qui en est fait. Ce que le photographe a su voir élargira et modifiera notre vision des choses. Un tel pouvoir cognitif doit être reconnu à une photo illustrant une annonce de parfums aussi bien qu'à une photo de mode ou à la vue panoramique d'un site de vacances. Une photo sportive ultra-rapide peut être un moyen de connaissance au même titre qu'une étude sophistiquée d'architecture, une nature morte ou le galbe d'une jambe.

Les photos noir-blanc et en couleurs réunies sur les pages qui suivent témoignent de la créativité d'un grand nombre de photographes connus et inconnus de nombreux pays. Cette sélection est ventilée par chapitres reconstituant grosso modo le cadre adéquat pour chaque cliché. Un tel principe de classification externe met en évidence la manière différenciée dont les photographes abordent leur tâche et cherchent à y apporter une solution optimale. C'est ainsi que ces séquences d'images respirent une atmosphère composite faite d'«états d'âme» fort variés: sobres ou imaginatives, stylistiquement sophistiquées ou nonchalantes, austères ou ludiques, statiques ou dynamiques, affectant un détachement de bon ton ou alors un engagement passionné, dures ou suaves, graves ou joyeuses, tout y passe. Au plan technique, elles peuvent s'avérer simples, réalisées sans aucune astuce optique ni technique; elles peuvent aussi bien recourir à tous les raffinements imaginables d'un appareil photo perfectionné, d'un choix astucieux de l'objectif ou de l'expérimentation en chambre noire et au labo.

Des différences de taille affectent surtout le comportement du photographe face à son sujet. Dans telle photo, il accentuera le message, l'expressivité aux dépens de la qualité technique. Dans telle autre, le perfectionniste en matière de technique s'en donnera à cœur joie. Les moyens stylistiques recouvrent eux aussi un large éventail, depuis le détail savamment élaboré en vertu d'un concept prédéterminé (et parfois vite testé à la Polaroïd) jusqu'à la forme visuelle jaillie de l'instinct, voire du hasard. Dans ces conditions, qui oserait attribuer la palme à l'un plutôt qu'à l'autre?

L'esthétique photographique comprend également ce qui n'apparaît pas dans l'image, ce qui en a été délibérément exclu, écarté ou omis: ainsi, tel mannequin inséré dans un espace vide chargé de mystère, tel autre par contre campé au sein d'un fourmillement d'objets évoquant la quotidienneté de la vie... Les photos aux accents formels accusés, parfois poussés jusqu'à un formalisme construc-

LA PHOTOGRAPHIE CONTRIBUE À ÉLARGIR NOTRE VISION DU RÉEL.

tiviste, s'opposent à des sujets en apparence tout à fait naturels qui posent néanmoins la question de savoir si le naturel n'est pas aussi étudié que la stylisation voulue. Le regard du photographe peut s'attacher à tel motif ou élément ou bien, au contraire, se perdre dans l'évocation épique de longue haleine.

A regarder des photos juste sorties des mains du photographe, préparées par le coordinateur de l'illustration, ou déjà incluses dans une campagne publicitaire ou une section de magazine, on se sent tiraillé entre deux attitudes contradictoires: faut-il plébisciter ce qui vous paraît conforme à votre propre tempérament et à votre goût personnel, ou alors accepter de vous identifier - avec le plaisir d'un voyeur - à ce qui vous paraît étrange,

autre et donc tentateur? Les photos réunies ici répondent à ces deux impulsions: elles satisfont la curiosité de l'amateur d'habituel et de traditionnel aussi bien que celle qu'attirent l'insolite, l'exotique, le non-raisonnable et l'aventureux.

Perspicace, Susan Sontag note dans ses réflexions «Sur la photographie» (On Photography, 1977) que «dans la mesure où la photographie débarrasse effectivement la vision traditionnelle de ses croûtes et scories, elle crée une nouvelle perception visuelle: intensive et détachée, engagée et distanciée à la fois, fascinée par le détail insignifiant tout comme par les dissonances. Il reste que la vision photographique doit être constamment rafraîchie par des chocs thématiques ou techniques nouveaux afin de maintenir la pression sur la rupture d'avec la vision traditionnelle. Provoquée par les révélations des photographes, la vision tend ainsi à s'adapter à la photographie.»

Il faut peut-être voir là la raison de notre besoin insatiable d'images photo toujours nouvelles, que nous consommons avec avidité. Les photos réunies dans le présent volume constituent à cet égard un viatique des plus appréciables.

WILLY ROTZLER, né en 1917 à Bâle, a passé son doctorat d'histoire de l'art à l'université de cette ville. De 1948 à 1961, conservateur du Musée des arts décoratifs de Zurich. De 1962 à 1968, rédacteur du magazine d'art Du; *depuis travaille comme critique d'art. A publié de nombreux livres, notamment des monographies (Johannes Itten, Camille Graeser, Friedrich Vordemberge-Gildewart, Arturo Bonfanti, Alberto Giacometti) ainsi que «Art et Graphisme», «Affiches politiques et sociales en Suisse», «Heinz Jost, affiches de théâtre». Nombreux articles parus dans les magazines* Du *et* Graphis.

■ **1–3** Photographs from a catalog issued by *Mimmina* for the fall/winter collection 1986/87. (ITA)

■ **1–3** Aufnahmen aus einem Katalog für die Herbst/Winter-Kollektion 1986/87 der Marke *Mimmina*. (ITA)

■ **1–3** Photos tirées d'un catalogue pour la collection automne/hiver 1986/87 de *Mimmina*. (ITA)

PHOTOGRAPHER:
Cheryl Koralik

CLIENT:
Mimmina

ART DIRECTOR:
Nando Miglio

AGENCY:
Modenese & Modenese

■ 1–3

PHOTOGRAPHER:
Barry Lategan

PUBLISHER:
Condé Nast S.p.A.

ART DIRECTOR:
Alberto Nodolini

■ 4—8

■ **4—8** "Something romantic on the holiday horizon" is the title of the fashion feature in *Vogue Italia*, to which these photos belong. *Alice in Wonderland* is the inspiration for these dresses that evoke memories of the aprons of yesteryear. (ITA)

■ **4—8** «Etwas Romantisches am Ferienhorizont» ist der Titel des Modebeitrags in *Vogue Italia*, zu dem diese Aufnahmen gehören. Lewis Carrolls *Alice im Wunderland* stand Pate für diese an schürzenartige Kinderkleidchen erinnernden Modelle. (ITA)

■ **4—8** Photos illustrant un article de mode dans *Vogue Italia* intitulé «Quelque chose de romantique à l'horizon des vacances». L'inspiration de Lewis Carroll (*Alice au pays des merveilles*) a prévalu dans ces modèles rappelant des petites robes-tabliers. (ITA)

PHOTOGRAPHER:
Uwe Ommer

PUBLISHER:
Martini Osvaldo

ART DIRECTOR:
Jean Yves Malbos
■ 11–15

■ **11–15** Photographs for the shoe collection by *Martini Osvaldo* for spring/summer 1986. Taken from a hardbacked catalog which comprises only full-page color photographs and the logo of the company. (ITA)

■ **11–15** Aufnahmen für die Schuhkollektion von *Martini Osvaldo* für Frühjahr/Sommer 1986. Der Katalog hat einen festen Einband und besteht ausschliesslich aus ganzseitigen Farbaufnahmen und dem Signet. (ITA)

■ **11–15** Photos pour la collection printemps/été 1986 qui réunit les créations du chausseur *Martini Osvaldo*. Le catalogue bénéficie d'une solide reliure. Il ne comporte que des illustrations couleurs pleine page et le logo de l'entreprise. (ITA)

■ **16** Example from a series of photographs for fashions created by *Amuleti*, published in *Vogue Italia*. (ITA)

■ **17, 18** The dress "Alimia", photographed by Horst (*17*) and "La Perla", photographed by Jeanloup Sieff (*18*); both for *Fujichrome* films, published in *Vogue Paris*, October 1985. (FRA)

■ **16** Beispiel aus einer in *Vogue Italia* veröffentlichten Serie von Aufnahmen für Mode von *Amuleti*. (ITA)

■ **17, 18** Das Kleid «Alimia», aufgenommen von Horst (*17*), und «La Perla», aufgenommen von Jeanloup Sieff (*18*); beide für *Fujichrome*-Filme, aus *Vogue Paris*, Oktober 1985. (FRA)

■ **16** Exemple tiré d'une série de photos de mode réalisée pour *Amuleti* et publiée dans *Vogue Italia*. (FRA)

■ **17, 18** Robe «Alimia», photographiée par Horst (*17*) et Body «La Perla», photographié par Jeanloup Sieff (*18*), les deux pour les films *Fujichrome*. *Vogue Paris*, Octobre 1985. (FRA)

PHOTOGRAPHER:
Paolo Roversi
CLIENT:
Mariella Burani per Amuletti
ART DIRECTOR:
Pitto Rondolotti
STUDIO:
Soncini & Ginepro
■ **16**

PHOTOGRAPHER:
Horst
PUBLISHER:
Condé Nast S.A.
CLIENT:
Fuji Film France
ART DIRECTOR:
Paul Wagner
■ **17**

PHOTOGRAPHER:
Jeanloup Sieff
PUBLISHER:
Condé Nast S.A.
CLIENT:
Fuji Film France
ART DIRECTOR:
Paul Wagner
■ **18**

Avec l'aimable autorisation de Fuji Film France.

Avec l'aimable autorisation de Fuji Film France.

■ **19—21** Full-page photographs from *Vogue Italia*. Tobago, the legendary island of Robinson Crusoe, is the subject which inspires these holiday fashions. (ITA)

■ **19—21** Ganzseitige Aufnahmen aus *Vogue Italia*. Hier geht es um Tobago, die legendäre Insel Robinson Crusoes, und entsprechend inspirierte Ferienmode. (ITA)

■ **19—21** Photos pleine page de *Vogue Italia*. On y présente l'île de Robinson Crusoé, Tobago, et une mode vacances inspirée de ce récit légendaire. (ITA)

PHOTOGRAPHER:
Albert Watson
PUBLISHER:
Condé Nast S.p.A.
ART DIRECTOR:
Alberto Nodolini
■ **19—21**

PHOTOGRAPHER:
Deborah Turbeville
PUBLISHER:
Condé Nast S.p.A.
ART DIRECTOR:
Alberto Nodolini
■ **25**

◀◀ P.P./S. 26/27
PHOTOGRAPHER:
Christin Losta
PUBLISHER:
Jardin des Modes
ART DIRECTOR:
Irma Schlumpf
STYLING:
Katharina Bébié-Lardelli
■ **24**

◀◀ Preceding spread:
■ **24** "Golden Romantic" is the title of the feature in *Jardin des Modes*, to which this photograph belongs. It relates to festive evening wear on a black and gold theme. (SWI)

■ **25** Photo from the "Beauty" section, with special reference to the subject of skin care, from the Italian *Vogue*. (ITA)

■ **26–28** Photographs from a promotion campaign for hosiery by *Evan-Picone*. (USA)

◀◀ Vorangehende Doppelseite:
■ **24** »Goldene Romantik« ist der Titel des Beitrags in *Jardin des Modes*, zu dem diese Aufnahme gehört. Es geht um festliche Abendmode, deren Thema Schwarz und Gold ist. (SWI)

■ **25** Aufnahme aus dem Schönheitssektor, hier speziell zum Thema Hautpflege, in der italienischen *Vogue*. (ITA)

■ **26–28** Aufnahmen aus einer Werbekampagne für Strümpfe der Marke *Evan-Picone*. (USA)

◀◀ Double page précédente:
■ **24** Photo illustrant l'article »Romantisme doré« dans un numéro du *Jardin des Modes*. Il y est question de grandes toilettes de soirée mariant le noir et l'or. (SWI)

■ **25** Photo pour la section »Beauté« de l'édition italienne de *Vogue*: il s'agit ici des soins de beauté pour la peau. (ITA)

■ **26–28** Photos illustrant une campagne publicitaire pour les bas *Evan-Picone*. (USA)

PHOTOGRAPHER:
Eric Michelson

CLIENT:
Evan-Picone Hosiery

ART DIRECTOR:
Eric Michelson

DESIGNER:
Eric Michelson

AGENCY:
Eric Michelson Design Inc.
■ 26—28

PHOTOGRAPHER:
David Bailey
PUBLISHER:
Condé Nast S.p.A.
ART DIRECTOR:
Alberto Nodolini
■ 30

PHOTOGRAPHER:
Tony Meneguzzo
PUBLISHER:
Condé Nast S.p.A.
ART DIRECTOR:
Alberto Nodolini
 31

PHOTOGRAPHER:
Paolo Roversi
CLIENT:
Romeo Gigli
ART DIRECTOR:
Pitto Rondolotti
AGENCY:
Soncini & Ginepro
■ 32

■ **30** Example from a series of photographs in *Vogue Italia.* High-fashion storm jackets worn over luxurious undergarments are presented. (ITA)

■ **31** Full-page photograph from a fashion feature in *Vogue Italia* entitled "Material and Form" dealing with various cashmere qualities. (ITA)

■ **32** Full-page photograph from an ad for fashions by *Romeo Gigli,* issued by *Vogue Italia.* (ITA)

■ **30** Beispiel aus einer Serie von Aufnahmen in *Vogue Italia.* Vorgestellt werden modische Windjacken, die über luxuriöser Wäsche getragen werden. (ITA)

■ **31** Ganzseitige Aufnahme aus einem Modeartikel in *Vogue Italia* unter dem Titel «Material und Form». Hier geht es um verschiedene Kaschmir-Qualitäten. (ITA)

■ **32** Ganzseitige Aufnahme aus einem Inserat für Mode von *Romeo Gigli,* erschienen in *Vogue Italia.* (ITA)

■ **30** Photo tirée d'une série publiée dans *Vogue Italia.* On y présente des blousons au goût du jour portés sur des dessous de luxe. (ITA)

■ **31** Photo pleine page pour un article de mode de *Vogue Italia* intitulé «Forme et matière». La matière en question, ce sont diverses qualités de cachemire. (ITA)

■ **32** Photo pleine page illustrant une annonce de mode pour *Romeo Gigli* parue dans *Vogue Italia.* (ITA)

PHOTOGRAPHER:
Neil Kirk
CLIENT:
Malisy
ART DIRECTOR:
Nando Miglio
AGENCY:
Nando Miglio S.r.L.
■ **33**

▶
PHOTOGRAPHER:
Douglas Hopkins
CLIENT:
Polaroid Corporation
ART DIRECTOR:
Marie McGinley
DESIGNER:
Marie McGinley
AGENCY:
Polaroid Corp./In House
■ **34**

■ **33** Photograph used for instore displays promoting fashion by the *Malisy* brand. (ITA)

■ **34** Photo from a promotion campaign for *"Polaroid* Professional Chrome" – the 4 x 5" transparency film, here targeted to fashion photographers; "something *perfectly* conventional." (USA)

■ **33** Für Laden-Displays verwendete Aufnahme, die für Mode der Marke *Malisy* wirbt. (ITA)

■ **34** Aufnahme aus einer Werbekampagne für den neuen 9 x 12 cm Diafarbfilm von *Polaroid,* hier speziell an Modephotographen gerichtet: «Etwas *perfekt* Konventionelles.» (USA)

■ **33** Photo pour la mode de la marque *Malisy,* exposée dans des magasins. (ITA)

■ **34** Photo pour une campagne *Polaroïd:* «quelque chose de *parfaitement* conventionnel» – le nouveau film inversible pour diapos couleur 9 x 12 cm, idéal pour la photo de mode. (USA)

PHOTOGRAPHER:
Conny Winter

CLIENT:
Kodak Ag

ART DIRECTOR:
Friedrich Müller

DESIGNER:
Conny Winter

AGENCY:
Kodak Ag/Werbeabt.

■ 35, 36

■ **35, 36** Photographs commissioned by *Kodak*, used for the Photokina-Profischau '86 in Cologne. (GER)

■ **35, 36** Im Auftrag von *Kodak* entstandene Aufnahmen, die für die Photokina–Profischau '86 in Köln verwendet wurden. (GER)

■ **35, 36** Photos réalisées pour le compte de *Kodak* et utilisées lors de la Photokina '86 de Cologne. (GER)

■ **37–40** Full-page photographs from a feature about holiday fashions in *Marie Claire*. Here the play of contrast between sun-tanned skin and black (*37, 38, 40*) and a pinafore. (FRA)

■ **37–40** Aufnahmen aus einem Beitrag über Ferienmode in *Marie Claire*. Hier das Spiel der Kontraste zwischen sonnenge-bräunter Haut und Schwarz (*37, 38, 40*) und eine Schürze. (FRA)

■ **37–40** D'un article de modes de vacances paru dans *Marie Claire*: modèles exemplifiant le jeu des contrastes que la peau en-tretien avec le noir (*37, 38, 40*) et un tablier. (FRA)

PHOTOGRAPHER:
Sacha

PUBLISHER:
Marie Claire

ART DIRECTOR:
Walter Rospert

■ **37–40**

PHOTOGRAPHER:
Sheila Metzner

CLIENT:
Bloomingdale's

ART DIRECTOR:
John C. Jay

DESIGNER:
John C. Jay/Ken Matsubara

AGENCY:
Bloomingdale's

■ **41–45**

■ **41–45** Photos from a large catalog issued by *Bloomingdale's* for the opening of "Boulevard Four" - a new department with international haute couture, perfumes and accessories. Shown are models by *Norma Walters* (41), *Chanel* (42), the cover photograph (43), *Ungaro's* perfume *Diva* (44) and *Ralph Lauren* (45). (USA)

■ **41–45** Aufnahmen aus einem grossformatigen Katalog des New Yorker Kaufhauses *Bloomingdale's* zur Eröffnung einer neuen Abteilung mit internationaler Haute-Couture, Parfums und Accessoires. Hier Modelle von *Norma Walters* (41), *Chanel* (42), das Umschlagphoto (43), *Ungaros Diva* (44) und *Ralph Lauren* (45). (USA)

■ **41–45** Photos tirées d'un catalogue au grand format des grands magasins newyorkais *Bloomingdale's*, pour un nouveau département de haute couture internationale (modes, parfums, accessoires): modèles de *Norma Walters* (41), *Chanel* (42), photo de couverture (43), le parfum *Diva d'Ungaro* (44) et *Ralph Lauren* (45). (USA)

PHOTOGRAPHER:
Sheila Metzner
CLIENT:
Bloomingdale's
ART DIRECTOR:
John C. Jay
DESIGNER:
John C. Jay/Ken Matsubara
AGENCY:
Bloomingdale's
■ 46

PHOTOGRAPHER:
Sheila Metzner

PUBLISHER:
Condé Nast Verlag GmbH

ART DIRECTOR:
Angelica Blechschmidt

■ **47, 48**

■ **46** From a large catalog issued by *Bloomingdale's* for the opening of "Boulevard Four" - a new department with international haute couture, perfumes and accessories. Shown is a model by *Nina Ricci* "Describing Deco: Evoking an Era". (USA)

■ **47, 48** Full-page photographs from a feature on fashion in the German *Vogue*: "Some like it cool." (GER)

■ **46** Aufnahme aus einem Katalog des New Yorker Kaufhauses *Bloomingdale's* zur Eröffnung einer neuen Abteilung mit internationaler Haute-Couture, Parfums und Accessoires. Hier ein Modell von *Nina Ricci* im Art-Déco-Stil. (USA)

■ **47, 48** Ganzseitige Aufnahmen aus einem Modebeitrag in der deutschen *Vogue*: »Manche mögen's cool.« (GER)

■ **46** Photo tirée d'un catalogue des grands magasins newyorkais *Bloomingdale's* pour un nouveau département de haute couture internationale (modes, parfums, accessoires). Ici un modèle art déco de *Nina Ricci*. (USA)

■ **47, 48** Photos pleine page pour un article de l'édition allemande de Vogue: «Certains l'aiment cool.» (GER)

■ **49** Photograph from a double-spread advertisement for fashions by *Blumarine.* From a campaign in *Vogue Italia.* (ITA)

■ **50** From a catalog for the fall/winter collection 1985/86 by *Gianni Versace,* as supplement to *Vogue Italia.* (ITA)

■ **49** Aufnahme aus einer doppelseitigen Anzeige für Mode von *Blumarine.* Aus einer Kampagne in *Vogue Italia.* (ITA)

■ **50** Aus einem Katalog für die Herbst/Winterkollektion 1985/86 von *Gianni Versace,* als Beilage von *Vogue Italia.* (ITA)

■ **49** Photo illustrant une annonce double page pour les modes *Blumarine.* Campagne lancée dans *Vogue Italia.* (ITA)

■ **50** Pour le catalogue automne/hiver 1985/86 des modes *Gianni Versace,* encarté dans *Vogue Italia.* (ITA)

PHOTOGRAPHER:
Albert Watson
CLIENT:
Blumarine
AGENCY:
Primo Punto
■ **49**

PHOTOGRAPHER:
David Bailey

CLIENT:
Gianni Versace

ART DIRECTOR
David Bailey

DESIGNER:
Werner

■ 50

PHOTOGRAPHER:
Albert Watson

CLIENT:
Blumarine

AGENCY:
Primo Punto

■ **52**

■ **52, 53** From a series of double-spread advertisements for fashions by *Blumarine*, appearing in *Vogue Italia*. (ITA)

■ **52, 53** Aus einer Serie von doppelseitigen Anzeigen für Mode von *Blumarine*, erschienen in *Vogue Italia*. (ITA)

■ **52, 53** D'une série d'annonces double page pour la mode *Blumarine*, publiée dans *Vogue Italia*. (ITA)

PHOTOGRAPHER:
Albert Watson

PUBLISHER:
Condé Nast S.p.A.

ART DIRECTOR:
Alberto Nodolini

■ 53

PHOTOGRAPHER:
Komaro Hoshino
PUBLISHER:
Popular Photography
ART DIRECTOR:
Shinichiro Tora
DESIGNER:
Shinichiro Tora
■ **54**

■ **54** Photograph from an editorial feature in *Popular Photography* published by CBS. (USA)

■ **55** "Evenings of Pure Magic" – this is the subject of the article in *Vogue Italia* to which this photograph belongs. (ITA)

■ **56** Full-page photograph from a series shot by internationally famous photographers (here by Francis Giacobetti) for *Kodachrome Professional Film*. (USA)

■ **54** Aufnahme aus einem redaktionellen Beitrag in *Popular Photography*, eine Zeitschrift von CBS. (USA)

■ **55** «Der Abend, ganz im Zeichen der Magie» ist das Thema des Beitrags in *Vogue Italia*, zu dem diese Aufnahme gehört. (ITA)

■ **56** Ganzseitige Aufnahme aus einer Serie von internationalen Photographen (hier von Francis Giacobetti) für *Kodachrome Professional Film*. (USA)

■ **54** Photo tirée d'un article du magazine *Popular Photography*, publié par CBS. (USA)

■ **55** «Des soirées emplies de magie» – c'est là l'intitulé de l'article de *Vogue Italia* illustré de cette photo. (ITA)

■ **56** Photo pleine page de Francis Giacobetti figurant dans une série réalisée pour le *Kodachrome Professional Film* par une équipe de grands photographes internationaux. (USA)

PHOTOGRAPHER:
David Bailey
PUBLISHER:
Condé Nast S.p.A.
ART DIRECTOR:
Alberto Nodolini
■ **55**

PHOTOGRAPHER:
Francis Giacobetti
PUBLISHER:
Eastman Kodak Co.
ART DIRECTOR:
Rolf Fricke
AGENCY:
Eastman Kodak Co.
■ **56**

PHOTOGRAPHER:
FABIO SANTAGIULIANA
PUBLISHER:
VICENZAORO
ART DIRECTOR:
FABIO SANTAGIULIANA
■ **57, 58**

■ **57, 58** Photographs in black and white from an editorial feature in the magazine *Vicenzaoro* about platinum jewellery. (ITA)

■ **57, 58** Aufnahmen in Schwarzweiss aus einem redaktionellen Beitrag in dem Magazin *Vicenzaoro* über Platin-Schmuck. (ITA)

■ **57, 58** Photos noir et blanc illustrant un article du magazine *Vicenzaoro* consacré aux bijoux de platine. (ITA)

PHOTOGRAPHER:
Rainer Bald
CLIENT:
H.I.S. Sportswear
ART DIRECTOR:
Feico Derschow
DESIGNER:
Feico Derschow
AGENCY:
RG Wiesmeier
■ 59

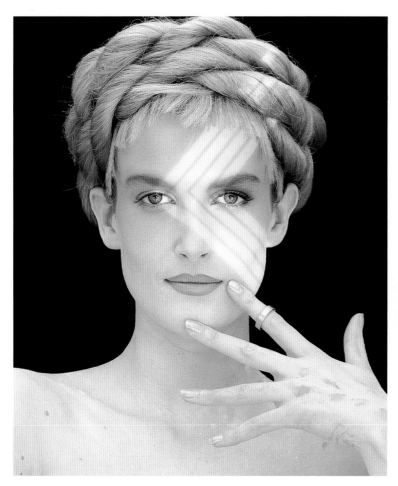 

PHOTOGRAPHER:
H.P. HOFFMANN

CLIENT:
NIESSING

ART DIRECTOR:
H.P.HOFFMANN

STUDIO:
H.P. HOFFMANN
■ **60, 61**

■ **59** "And they decided no longer to allow themselves to be fenced in and went over with flags flying to *h.i.s.*" Photograph from an ad for *h.i.s. sportswear.* The flag is used in shop windows and for in-store promotion. (GER)

■ **60, 61** Photographs from an advertising campaign for high-carat gold jewellery by *Niessing.* (GER)

■ **59** «Und sie beschlossen, sich durch nichts mehr einengen zu lassen, und liefen mit fliegenden Fahnen über zu *h.i.s.*» Aufnahme aus einem Inserat für *h.i.s. sportswear.* Die Fahne wird in Schaufenstern oder in Geschäften als Werbung verwendet. (GER)

■ **60, 61** Aufnahmen aus einer Anzeigenkampagne für hochkarätigen Goldschmuck von *Niessing.* (GER)

■ **59** «Et ils décidèrent de ne plus se laisser enserrer par quoi que ce soit et coururent se ranger sous le drapeau de *h.i.s.* Photo pour une annonce de *h.i.s. sportswear.* Le drapeau sert d'emblème publicitaire dans les vitrines et magasins. (GER)

■ **60, 61** Photos pour une campagne d'annonces en faveur des bijoux *Niessing* en or pur au titre élevé. (GER)

PHOTOGRAPHER:
Bob Murray

CLIENT:
Stride Rite Corp.

ART DIRECTOR:
Cheryl Heller

DESIGNER:
Cheryl Heller

AGENY:
HBM/Creamer Design Group

■ **63**

■ **63** Photograph for the front cover of the fall catalog for children's shoes by *Stride Rite*. (USA)

■ **64** Photograph for children's fashions, from a calendar. (USA)

■ **63** Aufnahme für die Umschlagvorderseiten des Herbstkatalogs für Kinderschuhe von *Stride Rite*. (USA)

■ **64** Aufnahme für Kindermode, aus einem Kalender. (USA)

■ **63** Photo pour la première page de couverture d'un catalogue de chaussures d'enfants *Stride Rite*. (USA)

■ **64** Photo de mode enfantine utilisée dans un calendrier. (USA)

PHOTOGRAPHER:
Marybeth Manarchy

CLIENT:
California Dreamers, Inc.

ART DIRECTOR:
James Lienhart

DESIGNER:
Joanne Genovese

AGENCY:
California dreamers, Inc.
■ 64

PHOTOGRAPHER:
Eric Michelson
CLIENT:
Robert Comstock
DESIGNER:
Yvon Dihe
AGENCY:
L'Agence
■ **65—69**

■ **65—69** The Natural History Museum in New York serves as the setting for sports fashion photos; also used for a self-promotion calendar by photographer Eric Michelson. (USA)

■ **65—69** Das naturhistorische Museum in New York diente hier als Kulisse für Sportmodeaufnahmen, die auch für einen Eigenwerbungskalender des Photographen verwendet wurden. (USA)

■ **65—69** Le Muséum d'histoire naturelle de New York a servi de coulisse à ces photos de modes sportives utilisées également dans un calendrier du photographe Eric Michelson. (USA)

PHOTOGRAPHER:
Hannes Schmid
PUBLISHER:
Condé Nast S.p.A.
ART DIRECTOR:
Armando Chitolina
■ 75

PHOTOGRAPHER:
Deborah Turbeville
PUBLISHER:
Condé Nast S.p.A.
ART DIRECTOR:
Alberto Nodolini
■ 74

■ **74** Full-page photograph from an article on perfumes under the "Beauty" section in the Italian edition of *Vogue*. (ITA)

■ **75** Black-and-white photo from the men's fashion magazine *L'Uomo* for a feature about nightwear and underwear. (ITA)

■ **74** Ganzseitige Aufnahme aus einem Beitrag über Parfums unter der Rubrik «Schönheit» in der italienischen *Vogue*. (ITA)

■ **75** Schwarzweiss-Aufnahme aus dem Herrenmode-Magazin *L'Uomo* für einen Beitrag über Nacht- und Unterwäsche. (ITA)

■ **74** Photo pleine page pour un article sur les parfums. Rubrique «Beauté» de l'édition italienne de *Vogue*. (ITA)

■ **75** Photo noir et blanc pour un article du magazine de modes masculines *L'Uomo* sur les sous-vêtements et les pyjamas. (ITA)

PHOTOGRAPHER:
Claus Wickrath

PUBLISHER:
Condé Nast S.p.A.

ART DIRECTOR:
Armando Chitolina
■ **76—78**

■ **76—78** Photographs from a fashion feature entitled "The Colors of the Forest" from the Italian fashion magazine for men *L'Uomo.* Shown here, a pullover and a jacket by *Chagall* (76) as well as a coat (77) and a jacket (78) by *Gerani Themen.* (ITA)

■ **76—78** Aufnahmen aus einem Modebeitrag unter dem Titel «Die Farben des Waldes» in dem Herrenmagazin *L'Uomo.* Hier für einen Pullover und eine Jacke der Marke *Chagall* (76), für einen Mantel (77) und eine Jacke (78) von *Gerani Themen.* (ITA)

■ **76—78** Photos illustrant un article de mode intitulé «Les Couleurs de la forêt» dans le magazine italien de modes masculines *L'Uomo:* pull et veste de la marque *Chagall* (76), manteau (77) et veste (78) de *Gerani Themen.* (ITA)

PHOTOGRAPHER:
Sheila Metzner

CLIENT:
Complice

ART DIRECTOR:
Nando Miglio

DESIGNER:
Art Works Alas

AGENCY:
Nando Miglio S.r.L.

■ **79, 80**

■ **79, 80** Photographs used for instore displays promoting fashion by the *Complice* brand. (ITA)

■ **79, 80** Für Laden-Displays verwendete Aufnahmen, die für Mode der Marke *Complice* werben. (ITA)

■ **79, 80** Photos pour la mode de la marque *Complice*, exposées dans des magasins. (ITA)

COSMETICS / KOSMETIK / COSMÉTIQUES

PHOTOGRAPHER:
Noriaki Yokosuka

CLIENT:
Shiseido Co. Ltd.

ART DIRECTOR:
Makoto Nakamura

DESIGNER:
Makoto Nakamura

■ 81

62

PHOTOGRAPHER:
Eric Michelson
CLIENT:
Charles of the Ritz
AGENCY:
Eric Michelson Design
■ **82**

■ **81** Photograph from a promotion campaign for perfume by the Japanese cosmetic firm *Shiseido*. (JPN)

■ **82** Photograph used as promotion for cosmetic products marketed by *Charles of the Ritz*. (USA)

■ **81** Aufnahme aus einer Werbekampagne für Parfums der japanischen Kosmetikfirma *Shiseido*. (JPN)

■ **82** Aufnahme aus einer Kampagne für kosmetische Produkte der Marke *Charles of the Ritz*. (USA)

■ **81** Photo d'une campagne de publicité pour les parfums de la firme japonaise de cosmétiques *Shiseido*. (JPN)

■ **82** Photo de publicité pour les produits cosmétiques de la marque *Charles of the Ritz*. (USA)

PHOTOGRAPHER:
Snowdon
PUBLISHER:
Condé Nast S.A.
ART DIRECTOR:
Paul Wagner
■ 83

PHOTOGRAPHER:
Hiro
PUBLISHER:
Condé Nast S.A.
ART DIRECTOR:
Paul Wagner
■ 84

PHOTOGRAPHER:
Jean Larivière
PUBLISHER:
Condé Nast S.A.
ART DIRECTOR:
Paul Wagner
■ 85

■ **83–85** Interpretations by internationally-acclaimed photographers of famous perfumes, from the French edition of *Vogue*. Shown here is the perfume "Madame Rochas" (*Rochas*), visualized by Snowdon (*83*); "Poison" (*Dior*), by Hiro (*84*); "First" (*Van Cleef & Arpels*), visualized by Jean Larivière (*85*) (FRA)

■ **83–85** Interpretationen berühmter internationaler Photographen von berühmten Parfums, aus *Vogue Paris*. Hier das Parfum «Madame Rochas» (*Rochas*), gesehen von Snowdon (*83*); «Poison» (*Dior*), gesehen von Hiro (*84*); und «First» (*Van Cleef & Arpels*), gesehen von Jean Larivière (*85*). (FRA)

■ **83–85** Interprétations de parfums célèbres par des photographes de renommée internationale, pour *Vogue Paris*. Ici, le parfum «Madame Rochas» (*Rochas*) vu par Lord Snowdon (*83*); «Poison» (*Dior*) vu par Hiro (*84*); «First» (*Van Cleef & Arpels*) vu par Jean Larivière (*85*). (FRA)

■ **86—89** Examples from a series of photographs of famous perfumes visualized by famous photographers (see also *83-85*) in *Vogue Paris.* Shown are "Dans la Nuit" (*Worth*), visualized by Jean-Frédéric Schall (*86*); "Ma Griffe" (*Carven*), visualized by Jeanloup Sieff (*87*); "1000" (*Patou*), by Nana Watanabe (*88*) and "Nocturnes" (*Caron*), by William Klein (*89*). (FRA)

■ **86—89** Beispiele aus einer Serie von Aufnahmen berühmter Parfums, visualisiert von berühmten Photographen (s. auch *83-85*), aus *Vogue, Paris.* Hier »Dans la Nuit« (*Worth*), von Jean-Frédéric Schall (*86*); »Ma Griffe« (*Carven*), von Jeanloup Sieff (*87*); »1000« (*Patou*), von Nana Watanabe (*88*) und »Nocturnes« (*Caron*), von William Klein (*89*). (FRA)

■ **86—89** Exemples d'une série de photos de parfums célèbres, vus par des photographes célèbres, parue dans *Vogue Paris* (cf. *83-85*). Ici, «Dans la Nuit» (*Worth*), vu par Jean-Frédéric Schall (*86*); «Ma Griffe» (*Carven*), vu par Jeanloup Sieff (*87*); «1000» (*Patou*), vu par Nana Watanabe (*88*) et «Nocturnes» (*Caron*), vu par William Klein (*89*). (FRA)

PHOTOGRAPHER:
Jean-Frédéric Schall
PUBLISHER:
Condé Nast S.A.
ART DIRECTOR:
Paul Wagner
■ **86**

PHOTOGRAPHER:
Jeanloup Sieff
PUBLISHER:
Condé Nast S.A.
ART DIRECTOR:
Paul Wagner
■ **87**

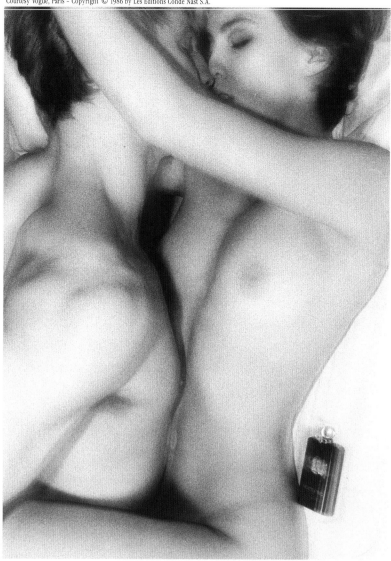

PHOTOGRAPHER:
Nana Watanabe

PUBLISHER:
Condé Nast S.A.

ART DIRECTOR:
Paul Wagner

 88

PHOTOGRAPHER:
William Klein

PUBLISHER:
Condé Nast S.A.

ART DIRECTOR:
Paul Wagner

■ 89

■ **90** "A perfume never comes alone." Double-spread photograph from an article in *Marie Claire* about products such as perfume-powders, perfume creams and perfume body lotions. (FRA)

■ **90** «Ein Parfum kommt niemals allein.» Doppelseitige Aufnahme aus einem Artikel in *Marie Claire* über Produkte wie Parfum-Puder, -Cremes und -Bodylotions. (FRA)

■ **90** «Un parfum ne vient jamais seul.» Photo double page d'un article de *Marie Claire* sur des poudres, crèmes et lotions parfumées pour le corps. (FRA)

PHOTOGRAPHER:
Sarah Moon

PUBLISHER:
Marie Claire

ART DIRECTOR:
Walter Rospert

■ **90**

PHOTOGRAPHER:
Harry DeZitter

CLIENT:
DeZitter Photography

ART DIRECTOR:
Harry DeZitter

DESIGNER:
Harry DeZitter

STUDIO:
DeZitter Photography

■ 91–94

■**91–94** From a self-promotion campaign for the DeZitter photo studio of New York. The photographs shown were shot in Maine, USA (*91* and *92*) and in Scotland – St. Andrews (*93*) and the Logie Bridge (*94*). (USA)

■**91–94** Aus einer Eigenwerbungskampagne für das Photostudio DeZitter, New York. Die Aufnahmen entstanden in Maine, USA (*91* und *92*) und in St. Andrews, Schottland, (*93*) sowie in Logie Bridge, Schottland (*94*). (USA)

■**91–94** Exemples d'une campagne autopromotionnelle du studio DeZitter à New York. Les photos ont été prises dans le Maine, USA (*91* et *92*), ainsi qu'à St. Andrews (*93*) et Logie Bridge (*94*), en Ecosse. (USA)

PHOTOGRAPHER:
Herbert W. Hesselmann
CLIENT:
Herbert W. Hesselmann
DESIGNER:
Herbert W. Hesselmann
■ **95**

■**95** Photo for an exhibition catalog of the Federation of Free-Lance Photo-Designers in Germany (BFF), published by the Union-Verlag, Stuttgart. The photograph (montage) served as motif for the month of August in a promotion calendar. (GER)

■**96** Photograph from an annual report for the *Valley National Bank* in Phoenix, Arizona. (USA)

■**95** Aus einem im Union-Verlag, Stuttgart, erschienenen Ausstellungskatalog für den Bund Freischaffender Foto-Designer in Deutschland (BFF). Die Aufnahme (eine Montage) diente als Kalendermotiv einer Gemeinschaftswerbung. (GER)

■**96** Für einen Jahresbericht der *Valley National Bank* in Phoenix, Arizona, aufgenommenes Photo. (USA)

■**95** D'un catalogue d'exposition d'une association allemande de photographes-designers indépendants (le BFF), publié aux éditions *Union.* La photo (un montage) est parue dans un calendrier, une publicité collective de plusieurs photographes. (GER)

■**96** Photo réalisée pour un rapport annuel de la *Valley National Bank* à Phoenix, Arizona. (USA)

PHOTOGRAPHER:
Rick Rusing

CLIENT:
Valley National Bank

ART DIRECTOR:
Steve Ditko

DESIGNER:
Shr Communications

AGENCY:
Shr Communications

■ 96

PHOTOGRAPHER:
Richard Misrach

PUBLISHER:
*Los Angeles County
Museum of Art*

ART DIRECTOR:
Richard Misrach

DESIGNER:
Deenie Yudell/Sandy Bell
■ **97, 98**

■ **97–100** Photos from *New American Photography*, an exhibition catalog issued by the Los Angeles County Museum of Art. Photographs *97* "Diving Board, Salton Sea" and *98* "Clothesline, Salton Sea" by Richard Misrach will appear in the book *Desert Cantos* to be published by University of New Mexico Press in 1987. *99* and *100* (using the entire 4x5" negative) are black-and-white photographs shot by Mark Klett in Arizona: "Plywood Tee-Pees" and "Bullet Riddled Saguaro". (USA)

■ **97–100** Aufnahmen aus dem Ausstellungskatalog *New American Photography* des Los Angeles County Museum of Art. Die Aufnahmen *97* «Sprungbrett» und *98* «Versunkene Wäscheleine» von Richard Misrach entstanden am Salton Sea in Kalifornien. Sie werden 1987 auch im Buch *Desert Cantos* (University of New Mexico Press) erscheinen. *99* und *100* (vollständige Verwendung der 4x5" Negative) wurden von Mark Klett in Arizona aufgenommen: «Sperrholz-Tipis» und «Kugeldurchlöcherter Säulenkaktus.» (USA)

■ **97–100** Photos du catalogue *New American Photography* publié par le Los Angeles County Museum of Art. Les photos *97* («Plongeoir») et *98* («Corde à linge submergée») de Richard Misrach proviennent de Salton Sea en Californie. Elles seront publiées en 1987 dans le livre *Desert Cantos* (University of New Mexico Press). Les photos *99* et *100* (format complet du négatif 4x5") sont prises par Mark Klett en Arizona: «Tipis en contre-plaqué» et «Cactus criblé de balles». (USA)

PHOTOGRAPHER:
Mark Klett
PUBLISHER:
Los Angeles County
Museum of Art
ART DIRECTOR:
Mark Klett
DESIGNER:
Deenie Yudell/Sandy Bell
■ **99, 100**

PHOTOGRAPHER:
Tom Bieber

CLIENT:
Burch Inc.

DESIGNER:
Steven Liska

AGENCY:
Liska & Associates, Inc.

■ **101**

■ **101** Shot of the car ferry on Lake Michigan for the November sheet of the 1986 calendar for Burch Inc. (printers). (USA)

■ **102** "Boat in the Reeds" is the title of this photo which appeared in the German edition of *Photo*. (GER)

■ **103** For the cover of an ad brochure about Walloon province and the city of Brussels. Issued by the Tourist Board. (BEL)

■ **101** Aufnahme einer Autofähre auf dem Lake Michigan für das Novemberblatt des Kalenders 1986 der Druckerei Burch Inc. (USA)

■ **102** «Boot im Schilf» ist der Titel dieser Aufnahme, erschienen in der deutschen Ausgabe der Fachzeitschrift *Photo*. (GER)

■ **103** Aufnahme für den Umschlag eines als Touristenwerbung verwendeten Prospekts über Wallonien und Brüssel. (BEL)

■ **101** Photo d'un bac sur le lac Michigan pour le calendrier 1986 (novembre) de l'imprimerie Burch Incorporated. (USA)

■ **102** Cette photo, parue dans l'édition allemande du magazine *Photo*, s'intitule «Bateau dans les roseaux». (GER)

■ **103** Photo pour la couverture d'un prospectus touristique sur la Wallonie et la ville de Bruxelles. (BEL)

PHOTOGRAPHER:
Fritz Dressler
PUBLISHER:
New Magazines
Verlagsgesellschaft mbh
ART DIRECTOR:
Thomas M. Schwan
■ 102

PHOTOGRAPHER:
Jean-Luc Deru/
Daylight s.p.r.l.
CLIENT:
O.P.T. Office De
Promotion du Tourisme
DESIGNER:
Béatrice Dujeux/
Jean-Luc Deru
■ 103

■ **104** Photo of a cat boat by Allan Weitz. (USA)

■ **105** Photo from "The Black and White Book" – a brochure issued by *Mead Paper*. The photographer is Terry Wild. (USA)

■ **104** Detail eines Kutters, aufgenommen von Allan Weitz. (USA)

■ **105** Aufnahme aus einer von *Mead Paper* herausgegebenen Broschüre «Das Schwarzweiss-Buch». (USA)

■ **104** Photo d'un cotre, prise par Allan Weitz. (USA)

■ **105** Photo de Terry Wild tirée d'une brochure publiée par *Mead Paper*, «Le livre noir et blanc». (USA)

PHOTOGRAPHER:
ALLAN WEITZ
■ **104**

PHOTOGRAPHER:
Terry Wild

CLIENT:
Mead Paper

AGENCY:
Corporate Graphics

■ 105

PHOTOGRAPHER:
John Snyder

CLIENT:
Brigham Young University

ART DIRECTOR:
McRay Magleby

DESIGNER:
McRay Magleby

AGENCY:
Byu Graphics

■ **106**

PHOTOGRAPHER:
Eberhard Grames/
Bilderberg

PUBLISHER:
Ellert & Richter Verlag

■ **107**

■ **106** From a brochure with philosophic texts and views, for the Brigham Young University – the largest private university in the USA, "North view from Carillon Tower." (USA)

■ **107** Photograph of the Zion Canyon in Utah for the photo-book "Untouched nature" published by *Ellert & Richter.* (GER)

■ **108** For the August sheet of the IBM 1986 calendar on the subject of Colorado and the concept "Quality". (USA)

■ **106** Aus einer Broschüre mit philosophischen Texten und Bildern für die Brigham Young University, die grösste private Universität der USA, «Ausblick vom Carillon-Turm nach Norden.» (USA)

■ **107** Aufnahme aus dem Zion Canyon in Utah für den Photoband *Unberührte Natur*, erschienen bei *Ellert & Richter.* (GER)

■ **108** Für das Augustblatt eines von IBM herausgegebenen Kalenders über Colorado und den Begriff «Qualität». (USA)

■ **106** «Au nord de la Tour du Carillon»: d'une brochure de la Brigham Young University, plus grande université privée américaine, illustrée de textes et photos philosophiques. (USA)

■ **107** Photo du Zion Canyon (Utah) pour un livre intitulé «Nature vierge», publié par *Ellert & Richter.* (GER)

■ **108** Feuillet d'août du calendrier 1986 publié par IBM, sur le Colorado et la notion de qualité. (USA)

PHOTOGRAPHER:
John Telford/
Stock Imagery

CLIENT:
IBM Corp.

ART DIRECTOR:
Tom Bluhm

AGENCY:
IBM Boulder
Design Center
■ 108

109 Photograph from an article in *Geo* entitled "The Untamed Monsters", on iceberg research. (GER)

110 For the book "Untouched Nature" (*Ellert & Richter*), a photograph shot in Breidarlón, Iceland. (GER)

111 Photograph of the Sinter terraces at Mammoth Hot Springs, taken from a book entitled "Fascination Landscape". (SWI)

109 Aufnahme aus einer Reportage in *Geo* über Eisbergforschung mit dem Titel «Die gezähmten Ungeheuer». (GER)

110 Für den Band *Unberührte Natur* (*Ellert & Richter*) verwendetes Photo, aufgenommen in Breidarlón, Island. (GER)

111 Aufnahme der Sinterterrassen von Mammoth Hot Springs (USA), aus dem Buch *Faszination Landschaft*. (SWI)

109 D'un reportage concernant la recherche sur les icebergs, intitulé «Les monstres apprivoisés», paru dans *Geo*. (GER)

110 Photo de Breidarlón en Islande, publiée dans «La nature vierge» (*Ellert & Richter*). (GER)

111 Photo des terrasses Sinter de Mammoth Hot Springs aux Etats-Unis, parue dans le livre «Fascination du paysage». (SWI)

PHOTOGRAPHER:
Klaus V. Mandelsloh/
Offshore Agency
PUBLISHER:
Gruner + Jahr Ag & Co.
ART DIRECTOR:
Erwin Ehret/
Franz Braun
■ **109**

PHOTOGRAPHER:
Eberhard Grames/
Bilderberg
PUBLISHER:
Ellert & Richter Verlag
■ **110**

PHOTOGRAPHER:
Max Schmid
PUBLISHER:
Verlag Photographie Ag
ART DIRECTOR:
Peter Wassermann
DESIGNER:
Peter Wassermann
■ 111

PHOTOGRAPHER:
Gail Mooney-Kelly
PUBLISHER:
*Travel & Leisure
Magazine*
ART DIRECTOR:
Adrian Taylor
■ 112

PHOTOGRAPHER:
Stephen O. Muskie

PUBLISHER:
Hoffmann & Campe

ART DIRECTOR:
Erika Schmied

■ 113

PHOTOGRAPHER:
Nathan Benn

PUBLISHER:
Hoffman & Campe

ART DIRECTOR:
Erika Schmied

■ 114

■ **112** Photograph taken in the old Silverado movie set outside of Santa Fe. Shot for a story on Santa Fé in *Travel & Leisure*. (USA)

■ **113, 114** From an issue of *Merian* magazine featuring the six New England states. *113* is a view of an abondoned farm in the North of Maine, *114* bird's eye view of Salisbury Beach, north of Cape Ann in Massachusetts. (GER)

■ **112** Die alte Western-Filmkulisse »Silverado« bei Santa Fe. Aus einem Artikel über Santa Fe in *Travel & Leisure*. (USA)

■ **113, 114** Aus einem *Merian*-Heft über Neu England, das aus sechs Staaten zwischen New York und Kansas besteht. *113* zeigt einen verlassenen Hof in Maine, *114* Salisbury Beach, nördlich von Cape Ann in Massachusetts, aus der Vogelperspektive. (GER)

■ **112** Photo des coulisses du Western »Silverado« tourné près de Santa Fe. D'un article sur Santa Fe dans *Travel & Leisure*. (USA)

■ **113, 114** D'un numéro de *Merian* sur la Nouvelle-Angleterre, qui comporte six états situés entre New York et le Kansas. *113* montre une ferme abandonnée au nord du Maine, *114* Salisbury Beach, au nord de Cape Ann, dans le Massachusetts. (GER)

PHOTOGRAPHER:
Dan Budnik
PUBLISHER:
Random House, Inc.
ART DIRECTOR:
Adelaide De Menil
■ **117, 119, 120**

■ **117-121** Photographs from *Men's Lives*, a book by Peter Matthiessen, published by *Random House*, about The Long Island (South Fork) Fishermen Project. *117* shows fisherman Stuart Vorpahl, *118* "Ocean haul – seine crew", *119* "Dory launching", *120* "Richard Wood setting up his trap", *121* "Tying on to haul the bag ashore." (USA)

■ **117–121** Aufnahmen für den im Verlag *Random House* erschienenen Band *Men's Lives* von Peter Matthiessen über ein Projekt für das Überleben der Fischerei auf Long Island. *117* zeigt den Fischer Stuart Vorpahl, *118* das Einbringen des Fischfangs, *119* ein schlingerndes Ruderboot, *120* Richard Wood beim Auslegen der Netze, *121* das Verankern zum Einbringen des Fangs. (USA)

■ **117–121** Photos pour *Men's Lives*, un livre de Peter Matthiessen consacré à un projet en faveur des pêcheurs de South Fork, Long Island, publié aux éditions *Random House*. Le numéro *117* montre le pêcheur Stuart Vorpahl, *118* la levée des filets, *119* le canot qui tangue, *120* Richard Wood tendant les filets, *121* l'ancrage pour tirer la pêche à terre. (USA)

PHOTOGRAPHER:
Lynn Johnson
PUBLISHER:
Random House, Inc.
ART DIRECTOR:
Adelaide De Menil
■ **118, 121**

PHOTOGRAPHER:
Klaus D. Francke/
Bilderberg
PUBLISHER:
DuMont Buchverlag
ART DIRECTOR:
W. Connertz
■ **122, 123**

■ **122, 123** Photographs from the large-size book *Iceland*, published by *DuMont* of Cologne. *122* shows a summer "Cloud Theater" in Kaldidalur, *123* the coast near Hvalnes Farm, Lönsfjörtur. Photographer Klaus D. Francke is founder member of the photographers' association Bilderberg, Hamburg. (GER)

■ **122, 123** Aufnahmen aus dem grossformatigen Band *Island*, erschienen im Verlag *DuMont*, Köln. *122* zeigt ein sommerliches «Wolkentheater» im Kaldidalur, *123* die Küste bei der Farm Hvalnes am Lönsfjörtur. Der Photograph Klaus D. Francke ist Gründungsmitglied der Photographenvereinigung Bilderberg. (GER)

■ **122, 123** Photos du grand volume *Islande*, publié chez *DuMont* à Cologne. La photo *122* montre un «théâtre de nuages» l'été à Kaldidalur, *123* la côte près de Farm Hvalnes au Lönsfjörtur. Le photographe Klaus D. Francke est membre fondateur de l'association de photographes Bilderberg, Hambourg. (GER)

ARCHITECTURE / ARCHITEKTUR

PHOTOGRAPHER:
Larry Olsen

CLIENT:
George Hyman
Construction Co.

ART DIRECTOR:
Ethel Kessler/
Ellen Roebuck

DESIGNER:
Ethel Kessler Design/
Ellen Roebuck

STUDIO:
Adams Studio, Inc.

■ **124**

PHOTOGRAPHER:
Larry Olsen

CLIENT:
*George Hyman
Construction Co.*

ART DIRECTOR:
*Ethel Kessler/
Ellen Roebuck*

DESIGNER:
*Ethel Kessler Design/
Ellen Roebuck*

STUDIO:
Adams Studio, Inc.

■ **125**

■ **124, 125** Photographs from a company brochure for George Hyman Construction Co. in which various building projects of the firm are shown. (USA)

■ **124, 125** Aufnahmen aus einer Firmenbroschüre des Bauunternehmens George Hyman Construction Co., in der verschiedene Bauprojekte der Firma gezeigt werden. (USA)

■ **124, 125** Photos d'une brochure d'entreprise de la firme George Hyman Construction, dans laquelle sont présentés divers projets de construction. (USA)

PHOTOGRAPHER:
Greg Murphey

PUBLISHER:
Anthony Russell, Inc.

ART DIRECTOR:
Anthony Russell

DESIGNER:
Casey Clark

AGENCY:
Anthony Russell, Inc.

■ **126**

PHOTOGRAPHER:
Richard Payne

CLIENT:
Polaroid Corp.

ART DIRECTOR:
Marie McGinley

DESIGNER:
Marie McGinley

AGENCY:
Polaroid Corp./In House

■ **127**

■ **126** Photograph within an article appearing in *U.S. Eye* about photographer Greg Murphey. Shown is the interior of the Mosque at King Kahlid Airport in Riyadh, Saudi Arabia. (USA)

■ **127** From an advertising campaign for the new conventionally processed 4x5" transparency film by *Polaroid*, here recommended especially for architectural photography. The building is "The Mesa" (architects: Arquitectonica) of Houston, Texas. (USA)

■ **126** Innerhalb eines Artikels über den Photographen Greg Murphey veröffentlichte Aufnahme in *U.S. Eye*. Hier das Innere der Moschee am King-Kahlid-Flughafen in Riad, Saudi-Arabien. (USA)

■ **127** Aufnahme aus einer Werbekampagne für den neuen 4x5"-Farbfilm von *Polaroid*, hier speziell für Architekturaufnahmen empfohlen. Das Gebäude ist «The Mesa» (Architekten: Arquitectonica) in Houston, Texas. (USA)

■ **126** Photo illustrant un article sur le photographe Greg Murphey, paru dans *U.S. Eye*. Ici, l'intérieur de la mosquée de l'aéroport King Kahlid à Riad, Arabie Saoudite. (USA)

■ **127** Photo d'une campagne de publicité pour la nouvelle pellicule couleurs 4x5" de *Polaroïd*, recommandée pour les photos d'architecture. Le bâtiment représenté est «The Mesa» (architectes: Arquitectonica) à Houston, Texas. (USA)

PHOTOGRAPHER:
Joe Baraban
CLIENT:
Adams & Porter
ART DIRECTOR:
Jay Loucks
AGENCY:
Loucks Atelier
■ **128**

■**128** Photograph for advertising purposes for *Adams & Porter* of Houston, Texas. (USA)

■**129** From an article in *Zeitmagazin* about the architect team "Arquitectonica" in Miami, who designed the famous "Hole of Miami"; an 11 square-meter-large space through an apartment house at the height of the twelfth floor. (GER)

■**130** The west façade of the New York State Capitol Building in Albany. For the montage the complete negative was used – which accounts for the marked frame. (USA)

■**128** Für Werbezwecke der Firma *Adams & Porter* in Houston, Texas, verwendete Aufnahme. (USA)

■**129** Aus einer Reportage im *Zeitmagazin* über das Architekten-Team «Arquitectonica» in Miami, welches das berühmte «Loch von Miami», einen 11 m² grossen Durchblick auf der Höhe des 12. Stockwerks eines Appartement-Hauses entwarf. (GER)

■**130** Die Westfassade des Regierungsgebäudes des Staates New York in Albany. Für die Montage wurde jeweils das vollständige Negativ verwendet, daher die Randmarkierungen. (USA)

■**128** Photo utilisée pour la publicité de *Adams & Porter*, une firme de Houston, Texas. (USA)

■**129** D'un reportage paru dans le *Zeitmagazin* sur le collectif d'architectes «Arquitectonica» de Miami, qui a conçu le fameux «trou de Miami», une trouée de 11 m² de surface à la hauteur de 12ᵉ étage d'un immeuble d'appartements. (GER)

■**130** Façade ouest du siège du gouvernement de l'Etat de New York à Albany. Pour le montage, le négatif complet a été utilisé, d'où les marques sur les bords. (USA)

PHOTOGRAPHER:
Dorothea Schwarzhaupt

PUBLISHER:
Zeitverlag
Gerd Bucerius Kg

ART DIRECTOR:
Christian Diener

■ 129

PHOTOGRAPHER:
Dan Weaks

CLIENT:
Lila Wallace Foundation

ART DIRECTOR:
Perry Choate

■ 130

PHOTOGRAPHER:
Layos Keresztes

CLIENT:
Knoll International

ART DIRECTOR:
Wolf Kaiser

DESIGNER:
Rudolf Beck

■ **131–133, 135–138**

PHOTOGRAPHER:
Holger Matthies

CLIENT:
Knoll International

ART DIRECTOR:
Wolf Kaiser

DESIGNER:
Rudolf Beck

■ **134**

■ **131–138** Examples from an advertising campaign for timeless furniture by *Knoll International.* The title of the furniture (which, with the exception of the *Humana* Collection, is named after its designer), and the country in which it was photographed, are both mentioned under the photograph. *131: Humana* office chair in Argentina; *132: Bertoia* chair in Brazil; *133: Aulenti* chair in Australia; *134: Humana* office chair in Indonesia; *135: Brno* chair in Morocco; *136: Humana* office chair in Luxemburg; *137: Saarinen* chair in Argentina; *138: Sottsass* chair in Egypt. (GER)

■ **131–138** Beispiele aus einer Anzeigen-Kampagne für zeitlose Möbel von *Knoll International.* Das (ausser bei der *Humana-* Collection) nach dem Möbel-Designer benannte Produkt und das Land, in dem es photographiert wurde, sind unter den Aufnahmen vermerkt. *131: Humana*-Bürosessel in Argentinien; *132: Bertoia*-Stuhl in Brasilien; *133: Aulenti*-Stuhl in Australien; *134: Humana*-Bürosessel in Indonesien; *135: Brno*-Sessel in Marokko; *136: Humana*-Bürosessel in Luxemburg; *137: Saarinen*-Sessel in Argentinien; *138: Sottsass*-Sessel in Ägypten. (GER)

■ **131–138** Exemples d'une campagne d'annonces pour les meubles indémodables de *Knoll International.* Sauf pour la collection *Humana*, les créations sont nommées d'après les designers. Les pays où les photos ont été prises sont indiqués. *131:* le siège de bureau *Humana* en Argentine; *132:* la chaise *Bertoia* au Brésil; *133:* la chaise *Aulenti* en Australie; *134:* le siège de bureau *Humana* en Indonésie; *135:* le fauteuil *Brno* au Maroc; *136:* le siège de bureau *Humana* au Luxembourg; *137:* le fauteuil *Saarinen* en Argentine; *138:* le fauteuil *Sottsass* en Egypte. (GER)

PHOTOGRAPHER:
Adriano Heitmann

PUBLISHER:
Ringier AG

ART DIRECTOR:
Adriano Heitmann

■ 139–141

■ **139–141** Photographs from an article in the magazine *Illustré* about the Ticinese architect Mario Botta. The photograph has created an unusual atmosphere for the furniture items by showing them with Japanese Butoh dancer Carlotta Ikeda. In *139* she pushes away the classic chair "Prima"; *140* shows the dancer with Botta's marble table "Terzo", *141:* the latest creation named "Quinta" induces the user to take a rather dignified upright posture. (SWI)

■ **139–141** Aufnahmen aus einer in der Zeitschrift *Illustré* erschienenen Reportage über den Tessiner Architekten Mario Botta, dessen Kreationen der Photograph auf ungewöhnliche Weise mit der japanischen Butoh-Tänzerin Carlotta Ikeda in Einklang gebracht hat. In *139* stösst sie den Klassiker unter den Stühlen, «Prima», von sich; *140* zeigt sie mit dem Marmortisch «Terzo»; *141* präsentiert die neuste Kreation, genannt «Quinta». (SWI)

■ **139–141** Photos d'un reportage sur les créations de meubles de l'architecte tessinois Mario Botta, paru dans le magazine *L'Illustré*. Le photographe a choisi un mode de présentation original, mettant en scène la danseuse japonaise de Butoh, Carlotta Ikeda. Sur la photo *139*, celle-ci repousse «Prima», une «idée» de chaise déjà vieillie; sur la photo *140* elle se trouve auprès de la table-autel en marbre «Terzo»; *141* présente la dernière-née, «Quinta». (SWI)

PHOTOGRAPHER:
Bruce Wolf

CLIENT:
Martex/
West Point Pepperell

ART DIRECTOR:
James Sebastian

DESIGNER:
James Sebastian/
Pen-Ek Ratanaruang

STUDIO:
Designframe
Incorporated

■ **142, 143**

■ **142, 143** Photograph for the cover, and a shot from the inside pages of a catalog for *Martex* home textiles entitled "The Art of *Martex*." (USA)

■ **142, 143** Aufnahme für den Umschlag und eine Aufnahme aus dem Inhalt eines Katalogs für *Martex*-Heimtextilien mit dem Titel «Die Kunst von *Martex*». (USA)

■ **142, 143** Photo de couverture et un exemple du contenu d'un catalogue des tissus d'ameublement *Martex*, intitulé «L'art de *Martex*». (USA)

PEOPLE / MENSCHEN / PERSONNES

PHOTOGRAPHER:
GIUSEPPE PINO
PUBLISHER:
CONDÉ NAST S.P.A.
ART DIRECTOR:
ALBERTO NODOLINI

■ **144**

■ **144** Photo from a regularly appearing series in *Vogue Italia* entitled "Artists in the Studio"; shown is a portrait of New York painter Helen Frankenthaler. (ITA)

■ **145, 146** Full-page photos from a feature on Milan's famous designers, in *Merian*. Shown are: (*145*) Alessandro Mendini in his "Studio Alchymia" and (*146*) Ettore Sottsass (founder of the Memphis Group). (GER)

■ **144** Aufnahme aus einer regelmässig in *Vogue Italia* erscheinenden Serie mit dem Titel «Künstler im Atelier», hier ein Porträt der New Yorker Malerin Helen Frankenthaler. (ITA)

■ **145, 146** Ganzseitige Aufnahmen aus einem Beitrag über Mailands Designer in *Merian*, hier (*145*) Alessandro Mendini in seinem «Studio Alchymia» und (*146*) Ettore Sottsass, Gründer der Gruppe «Memphis». (GER)

■ **144** D'une série intitulée «Artistes dans l'atelier», publiée périodiquement dans *Vogue Italia*: portrait de la femme peintre newyorkaise Helen Frankenthaler. (ITA)

■ **145, 146** Photos pleine page d'un reportage sur les designers milanais paru dans *Merian*. Ici, Alessandro Mendini (*145*) dans son «Studio Alchymia» et Ettore Sottsass (*146*), fondateur du groupe «Memphis». (GER)

PHOTOGRAPHER:
Aldo Ballo
PUBLISHER:
Hoffmann & Campe
ART DIRECTOR:
Erika Schmied
■ 145

PHOTOGRAPHER:
Aldo Ballo
PUBLISHER:
Hoffmann & Campe
ART DIRECTOR:
Erika Schmied
■ 146

PHOTOGRAPHER:
Tom Zimberoff

CLIENT:
Tom Zimberoff

ART DIRECTOR:
Tom Zimberoff

DESIGNER:
Craig Butler/
Butler Advertising

■ **147**

147 Portrait of General Chuck Yeager with a WWII vintage P-51 *Mustang* fighter plane photographed by Tom Zimberoff for a self-promotional brochure called the "Pocketfolio". (USA)

148 Portrait of American painter James Rosenquist from an article in the *Frankfurter Allgemeine Magazin.* (GER)

149 From an article about Harold Edgerton, inventor of high speed photography (stroboscope flash), in the *Frankfurter Allgemeine Magazin.* (GER)

147 Porträt von General Chuck Yeager mit einer WWII P-51 *Mustang*, aufgenommen von Tom Zimberoff für seine Eigenwerbungsbroschüre «Pocketfolio». (USA)

148 Porträt des amerikanischen Malers James Rosenquist aus einem Artikel im *Frankfurter Allgemeine Magazin.* (GER)

149 Aufnahme aus einem Beitrag über Harold Edgerton, Erfinder des Stroboskopblitzes in der Photographie, im *Frankfurter Allgemeine Magazin.* (GER)

147 Portrait du Général Chuck Yeager avec l'ancien WWII P-51 *Mustang*, tiré d'une brochure «Pocketfolio» du photographe Tom Zimberoff. (USA)

148 Portrait du peintre américain James Rosenquist illustrant un article du *Frankfurter Allgemeine Magazin.* (GER)

149 Photo d'un article du *Frankfurter Allgemeine Magazin* sur Harold Edgerton, inventeur du flash stroboscope appliqué à la photographie. (GER)

PHOTOGRAPHER:
ABE FRAJNDLICH
PUBLISHER:
FRANKFURTER ALLGEMEINE ZEITUNG GMBH
ART DIRECTOR:
HANS-GEORG POSPISCHIL
■ **148**

PHOTOGRAPHER:
ABE FRAJNDLICH
PUBLISHER:
FRANKFURTER ALLGEMEINE ZEITUNG GMBH
ART DIRECTOR:
HANS-GEORG POSPISCHIL
■ **149**

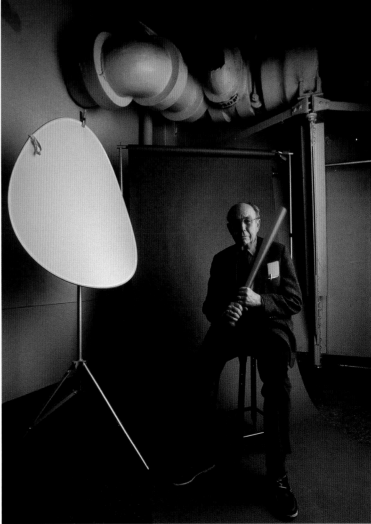

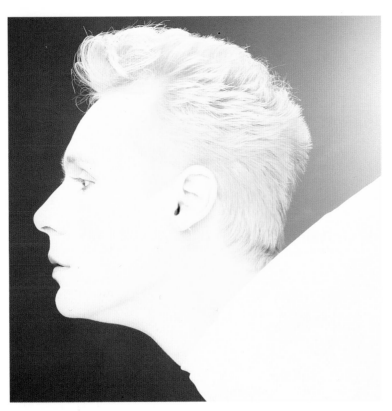

PHOTOGRAPHER:
Beverly Parker

PUBLISHER:
CBS Inc.

ART DIRECTOR:
Allen Weinberg

DESIGNER:
Allen Weinberg

STUDIO:
CBS Records
■**150**

PHOTOGRAPHER:
William Coupon

PUBLISHER:
Dansen Magazine
■**151**

■**150** Portrait of pop singer and guitarist Digney Fignus for a CBS record. (USA)

■**151** Fashion portrait with Wynton Marsalis (jazz and classical trumpet) about fashion designer Issey Miyake in the Japanese magazine *Dansen.* (JPN)

■**152** Double-spread photograph from a feature on drummer Art Blakey, in the *Frankfurter Allgemeine Magazin.* (GER)

■**150** Porträt des Pop-Sängers und Gitarristen Digney Fignus für eine bei CBS erschienene Schallplatte. (USA)

■**151** Modeporträt mit Wynton Marsalis (Jazz und klassische Trompete) aus einem Beitrag über den Modeschöpfer Issey Miyake in der japanischen Zeitschrift *Dansen.* (JPN)

■**152** Aufnahme aus einem Bericht über den Schlagzeuger Art Blakey im *Frankfurter Allgemeine Magazin.* (GER)

■**150** Portrait du chanteur pop et guitariste Digney Fignus pour un disque paru chez CBS. (USA)

■**151** Portrait de mode avec Wynton Marsalis (trompette jazz et classique) illustrant un article sur le modéliste Issey Miyake, publié dans le magazine japonais *Dansen.* (JPN)

■**152** Photo double page d'un reportage sur le batteur Art Blakey, paru dans le *Frankfurter Allgemeine Magazin.* (GER)

PHOTOGRAPHER:
Abe Frajndlich
PUBLISHER:
*Frankfurter Allgemeine
Zeitung GmbH*
ART DIRECTOR:
Hans-Georg Pospischil
■ 152

PHOTOGRAPHER:
Dmitri Kasterine
■ **154**

PHOTOGRAPHER:
Scott Heiser
■ 155

■ **154** Portrait of artist Julian Schnabel, New York, 1986. (USA)   ■ **154** Porträt des Malers Julian Schnabel, New York, 1986. (USA)   ■ **154** Portrait de l'artiste Julian Schnabel, New York. (USA)

■ **155** Personal study by photographer Scott Heiser. (USA)   ■ **155** Persönliche Studie des Photographen Scott Heiser. (USA)   ■ **155** Etude par le photographe Scott Heiser. (USA)

■ **156—161** Portraits of celebrities in American film by photographer Terry O'Neill. Shown is Ginger Rogers *(156)*, Elizabeth Taylor *(157)*, Roy Rogers and Dale Evans *(158)*, producer Richard Zanuck and his wife Lili *(159)*, Fred Astaire *(160)* and one time film stars L. Gish and D. Fairbanks, Jr. *(161)*. (USA)

■ **156—161** Porträts von Berühmtheiten des amerikanischen Films, aufgenommen von Terry O'Neill. Hier Ginger Rogers *(156)*, Elizabeth Taylor *(157)*, Roy Rogers und Dale Evans *(158)*, Produzent Richard Zanuck und seine Frau Lili *(159)*, Fred Astaire *(160)* und Altstars: L. Gish und D. Fairbanks, Jr. *(161)*. (USA)

■ **156—161** Portraits de célébrités du cinéma américain réalisés par le photographe Terry O'Neill. La photo *156* montre Ginger Rogers, *157* Elizabeth Taylor, *158* Roy Rogers et Dale Evans, *159* le producteur Richard Zanuck et sa femme Lili, *160* Fred Astaire et *161* les vedettes d'autrefois L. Gish et D. Fairbanks Jr. (USA)

PHOTOGRAPHER:
Klaus Bossemeyer/
Bilderberg
PUBLISHER:
Ellert & Richter
Verlag
■ **162, 163**

■ **162, 163** Full-page and double-spread photo from a book entitled *Toskana* (Tuscany), published by *Ellert & Richter*. Shown is
a butcher from Prato, the town at the foot of the Apennines (*162*)
and a store in which everything necessary for Tuscan cuisine is
stocked. Managed by mother and daughter, it is located in Radda –
the heart of the Chianti district (*163*). (GER)

■ **162, 163** Ganzseitige und doppelseitige Aufnahme aus einem
Buch mit dem Titel *Toskana*, erschienen bei *Ellert & Richter*. Hier
ein Metzger aus Prato, der Stadt am Fusse des Apennin (*162*), und
ein von Mutter und Tochter geführter Laden in Radda, mitten im
Chianti-Gebiet, wo man alles kaufen kann, was die toskanische
Küche verlangt (*163*). (GER)

■ **162, 163** Photos pleine page et double page d'un livre intitulé
Toskana («Toscane») paru chez *Ellert & Richter*, Hambourg. Ici,
un boucher de Prato, une ville située au pied des Apennins (*162*)
et un magasin tenu par une mère et sa fille à Radda, en pleine
région du Chianti: on y trouve tout ce qui est nécessaire à la cuisine toscane (*163*). (GER)

PHOTOGRAPHER:
Jay Maisel

PUBLISHER:
Eastman Kodak Co.

ART DIRECTOR:
Rolf Fricke

■ **164**

PHOTOGRAPHER:
Eddie Adams

PUBLISHER:
William Collins
Sons & Co. Ltd.

ART DIRECTOR:
Leslie Smolan

DESIGNER:
Leslie Smolan/
Thomas Walker

AGENCY:
Carbone Smolan
Associates

■ **165**

■ **164** "French Man with Swiss Cheese" is the title of this portrait which appeared in an article about Jay Maisel in *International Photography* (*Kodak*). (USA)

■ **165** Full-page photograph from the book *A Day in the Life of Japan*. Shown is a portrait of 82-year-old artist Myoshin Nakamura from Aikawa. The Chinese letters painted by her in the background mean "Love". (JPN)

■ **166** Photograph commissioned by *Data General* and which was also used as self promotion by photographer Al Fisher. (USA)

■ **164** «Franzose mit Schweizer Käse» ist der Titel dieses Porträts, das innerhalb eines Artikels über Jay Maisel in *International Photography* (*Kodak*) veröffentlicht wurde. (USA)

■ **165** Ganzseitige Aufnahme aus dem Buch *A Day in the Life of Japan* («Ein Tag im Leben von Japan»). Es ist das Porträt der 82jährigen Künstlerin Myoshin Nakamura aus Aikawa. Die von ihr auf den Hintergrund gemalten Zeichen bedeuten «Liebe». (JPN)

■ **166** Im Auftrag von *Data General* entstandene Aufnahme von Al Fisher, die auch als Eigenwerbung verwendet wurde. (USA)

■ **164** «Français et fromage suisse» s'intitule ce portrait publié dans *International Photography* (*Kodak*) pour accompagner un article sur Jay Maisel. (USA)

■ **165** Photo pleine page tirée du livre *A Day in the Life of Japan*. Il s'agit ici du portrait de Myoshin Nakamura, une artiste de 82 ans d'Aikawa. A l'arrière-plan, une de ses calligraphies, qui signifie «Amour». (JPN)

■ **166** Photo réalisée par Al Fisher pour une commande de *Data General*. Elle sert également d'autopromotion. (USA)

PHOTOGRAPHER:
Al Fisher

CLIENT:
*Data General/
Al Fisher*

ART DIRECTOR:
Mark Kent

DESIGNER:
Mark Kent

AGENCY:
*Cipriani
Advertising, Inc.*

■ 166

PHOTOGRAPHER:
William Coupon

PUBLISHER:
Twa Ambassador

ART DIRECTOR:
Barbara Koster

DESIGNER:
Barbara Koster

■ **167–171**

■ **167–171** Examples of a series headed "Dutch Portraits" for the inflight magazine *TWA Ambassador*. William Coupon went on the trail of the great Dutch masters for his "Social Studies Twelve; The Traditional Dutch" and took shots in some of Holland's outlandish places, where traditional costume is still worn. (USA)

■ **167–171** Beispiele aus einer Serie von Porträts, die unter dem Titel «Holländische Porträts» in dem Flugmagazin *TWA Ambassador* erschienen. Auf den Spuren der grossen holländischen Meister nahm William Coupon Menschen in kleinen Orten Hollands auf, wo noch heute die traditionellen Trachten getragen werden. (USA)

■ **167–171** «Portraits de Hollande»: exemples d'une série parue dans le magazine de la compagnie aérienne TWA. Sur les traces des grands maîtres hollandais, William Coupon a photographié divers individus dans des régions où l'on porte encore aujourd'hui le costume traditionnel. (USA)

PHOTOGRAPHER:
Burkhard von Harder
PUBLISHER:
Zeitverlag
Gerd Bucerius Kg
ART DIRECTOR:
Christian Diener
■ 172–175

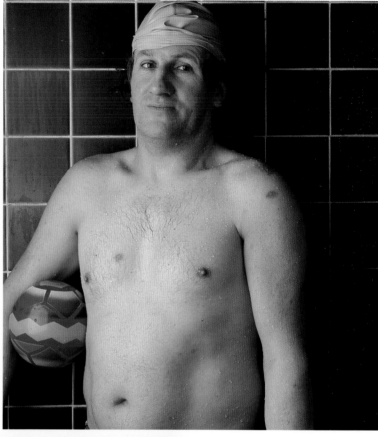

■**172–175** People in the swimming bath, from an article in *Zeitmagazin. 175* shows clearly that the compulsory cold shower has the same effect on adults and children. (GER)

■**172–175** Menschen im Schwimmbad, aus einem Beitrag im *Zeitmagazin*. Bei *175* wird deutlich, dass die obligatorische kalte Dusche für Gross und Klein die gleiche Wirkung hat. (GER)

■**172–175** Scènes de piscine pour un article du *Zeitmagazin*. Sur la photo *175*, on voit que la douche froide obligatoire fait le même effet aux grands qu'aux petits. (GER)

PHOTOGRAPHER:
Ron Schwenger/I·Media
PUBLISHER:
William Collins
Sons & Co. Ltd.
ART DIRECTOR:
Leslie Smolan
DESIGNER:
Leslie Smolan/
Tom Walker
AGENCY:
Carbone Smolan
Associates
■ 176

PHOTOGRAPHER:
Cindy Bellamy
PUBLISHER:
William Collins
Sons & Co. Ltd.
ART DIRECTOR:
Leslie Smolan
DESIGNER:
Leslie Smolan
AGENCY:
Carbone Smolan
Associates
■ 177

PHOTOGRAPHER:
GAIL MOONEY-KELLY
■ 178

■ **176, 177** Photos from the official book of the 100th Anniversary Celebration of Vancouver - *Vancouver: A Year in Motion*. *176* shows urban artist Robert Wyland putting the finishing touches to "Orcas", one of a series of whaling murals. It measures 30,4 x 213,4 meters and decorates the East wall of a seven story office block in Vancouver. *177* shows Vancouver's marine abundance in a shop window of a fish store. (CAN)

■ **178** "Sioux Lady" in a traditional dress. She had made it herself and had just been awarded the first prize at the prestigious annual Indian Market in Santa Fe. (USA)

■ **176, 177** Aufnahmen aus dem offiziellen Buch zur Hundertjahrfeier von Vancouver, *Vancouver: A Year in Motion*. *176* zeigt ein Wandbild mit Walen vor der Fertigstellung durch den Künstler Robert Wyland. Es misst 30,4 x 213,4 m und schmückt die Ostwand eines siebenstöckigen Bürogebäudes in Vancouver. *177* zeigt die reichhaltigen Gaben des Meeres im Schaufenster eines Fischgeschäftes. (CAN)

■ **178** Sioux-Indianerin in traditioneller Kleidung. Für diese selbstgemachte Tracht hatte sie gerade den ersten Preis beim jährlichen Indianer-Markt in Sante Fe erhalten. (USA)

■ **176, 177** Photos figurant dans le livre officiel du centenaire de la ville de Vancouver, *Vancouver: A Year in Motion*. La photo *176* montre Robert Wyland mettant la dernière main à une peinture murale représentant des baleines. Celle-ci mesure 30,4 x 213,4 m et orne le mur est d'un immeuble de bureaux de sept étages à Vancouver. La photo *177* montre les riches produits de la mer dans la vitrine d'une poissonnerie. (CAN)

■ **178** Femme sioux en costume traditionnel. Elle vient d'obtenir le premier prix pour son costume fait main au grand marché annuel des Indiens de Santa Fe. (USA)

PHOTOGRAPHER:
Jean Mézière
PUBLISHER:
Verlag Photographie Ag
ART DIRECTOR:
Peter Wassermann
■ 179

■ **179** Example from one of the series dedicated to nude photography in the open air by Jean Mézière, published in *Portfolio Photographie*. (SWI)

■ **180** Example of a nude photograph from the "red series" by Sepp von Mentlen, presented in *Portfolio Photographie*. (SWI)

■ **179** Beispiel aus einer in *Portfolio Photographie* veröffentlichten Serie von Jean Mézière, die der Aktphotographie im Freien gewidmet ist. (SWI)

■ **180** Beispiel einer Aktaufnahme aus der «roten Serie» von Sepp von Mentlen, in *Portfolio Photographie*. (SWI)

■ **179** Exemple d'une série de Jean Mézière consacrée à la photographie de nus en plein air qui a été publiée dans *Portfolio Photographie*. (SWI)

■ **180** Photo de la «série rouge» de Sepp von Mentlen, présentée dans *Portfolio Photographie*. (SWI)

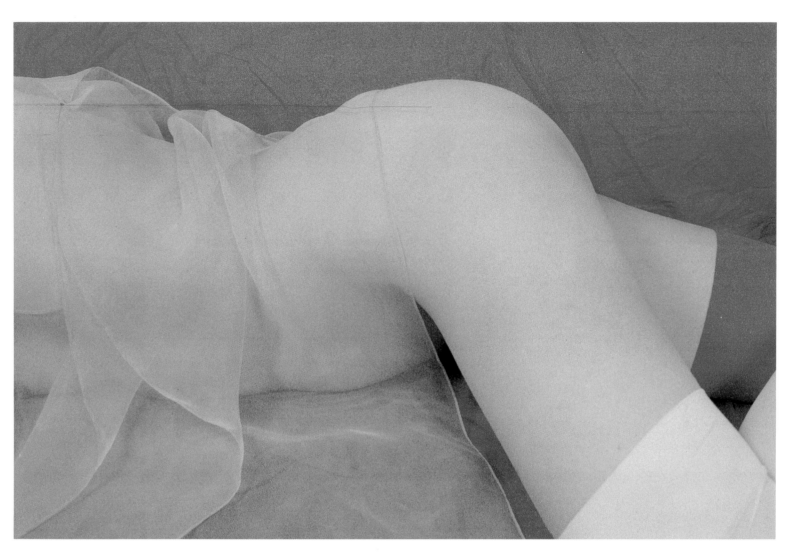

PHOTOGRAPHER:
Sepp von Mentlen
PUBLISHER:
Verlag Photographie Ag
ART DIRECTOR:
Peter Wassermann
■ 180

■ **182** Photo for the cover sheet of a hanging calendar which serves as joint promotion for the participants. (CAN)

■ **183** Example from a black-and-white nude series by Wolfhard Koeppe, taken with a panorama camera. Presented in *Portfolio Photographie*. (SWI)

■ **184** Photo done with infrared film by Roger Freeman, teacher of photography at Alfred University. From a brochure issued by the university. (USA)

■ **182** Aufnahme für das Deckblatt eines Wandkalenders, der als Gemeinschaftswerbung der Beteiligten diente. (CAN)

■ **183** Beispiel aus einer Schwarzweiss-Aktserie von Wolfhard Koeppe, aufgenommen mit einer Panoramakamera. Vorgestellt in *Portfolio Photographie*. (SWI)

■ **184** Mit Infrarotfilm gemachte Aufnahme von Roger Freeman, der an der Alfred University Photographie lehrt. Aus einer Broschüre der Universität. (USA)

■ **182** Photo pour la page de couverture d'un calendrier mural qui sert de publicité collective aux participants. (CAN)

■ **183** Exemple d'une serie de nus en noir et blanc de Wolfhard Koeppe, pris à l'aide d'un objectif panoramique. Photo présentée dans *Portfolio Photographie*. (SWI)

■ **184** Photo de Roger Freeman, réalisée avec une pellicule à infra-rouge, pour une brochure de l'Alfred University où celui-ci enseigne la photographie. (USA)

PHOTOGRAPHER:
Daniel Wiener
CLIENT:
Daniel Wiener
Eskind Waddell
Cooper & Beatty, Ltd.
Graphic Specialties Ltd.
MacKinnon-Moncur Ltd.
ART DIRECTOR:
Malcolm Waddell
DESIGNER:
Malcolm Waddell
AGENCY:
Eskind Waddell
■ **182**

PHOTOGRAPHER:
Wolfhard Koeppe
PUBLISHER:
Verlag Photographie Ag
ART DIRECTOR:
Peter Wassermann
■ 183

PHOTOGRAPHER:
Roger Freeman
CLIENT:
Alfred University
ART DIRECTOR:
Domenica Genovese/
James Hackley
DESIGNER:
Domenica Genovese/
James Hackley
STUDIO:
Roger Freeman
■ 184

PHOTOGRAPHER:
Peter Bersch
PUBLISHER:
Verlag Photographie Ag
ART DIRECTOR:
Peter Wassermann
■ **185**

■ **185** From a series of photographs entitled "Eva". The photographer experiments with old reproduction techniques; the photo shown here belongs to the realm of so-called high-fidelity print processes. From *Photographie*. (SWI)

■ **186** *Polaroid* photo from a series which has continued for 5 years by photographer Reza Khatir, who works preferably with instant-picture material. From *Portfolio Photographie*. (SWI)

■ **185** Aus einer Serie von Aufnahmen mit dem Titel «Eva». Der Photograph experimentiert mit alten Wiedergabetechniken; die hier gezeigte Aufnahme gehört in den Bereich der sogenannten Edeldruckverfahren. Aus *Photographie*. (SWI)

■ **186** *Polaroid*-Aufnahme aus einer seit 5 Jahren fortgesetzten Serie des Photographen Reza Khatir , der bevorzugt mit Sofortbild- material arbeitet. Aus *Portfolio Photographie*. (SWI)

■ **185** Exemple d'une série de photos intitulée «Eve». Le photographe expérimente de vieilles techniques de reproduction; cette photo, publiée dans *Photographie*, fait appel à des procédés de façonnage de luxe. (SWI)

■ **186** Photo *Polaroïd* d'une série réalisée sur 5 ans, parue dans *Portfolio Photographie*. Reza Khatir travaille de préférence sur du matériel photographique instantané. (SWI)

PHOTOGRAPHER:
Reza Khatir/Skylite
PUBLISHER:
Verlag Photographie Ag
ART DIRECTOR:
Peter Wassermann
■ 186

PHOTOGRAPHER:
Mark Ferri
PUBLISHER:
Connoisseur Magazine
ART DIRECTOR:
Carla Barr
■ 187

PHOTOGRAPHER:
Mark Ferri
PUBLISHER:
Metropolitan Home Magazine
ART DIRECTOR:
Mike Jensen
■ 188

PHOTOGRAPHER:
MARK FERRI
■189

■**187-189** Portrait photographs by Mark Ferri; shown here is: (187) Max Gordon, proprietor of the famous night club The Village Vanguard in New York, published in an article in *Connoisseur; 188* shows Milton Glaser in the Aurora restaurant, which he designed; *189* Albert Montano from Manhattan's Little Italy district. (USA)

■**187–189** Porträtaufnahmen des Photographen Mark Ferri; hier (187) Max Gordon, Besitzer des berühmten Nachtclubs The Village Vanguard in New York, veröffentlicht in einem Artikel in *Connoisseur;* (188) Designer Milton Glaser im Aurora Restaurant, das er eingerichtet hat; (189) Albert Montano aus Little Italy. (USA)

■**187–189** Portraits du photographe Mark Ferri: Max Gordon (187), propriétaire du célèbre night-club The Village Vanguard à New York, photo publiée dans le *Connoisseur;* Milton Glaser (188) au Aurora Restaurant et Albert Montano (189), habitant du quartier Italien de Manhattan (Little Italy). (USA)

■**190** Portrait of Asiatic nuns, used as self promotion for photographer Lee Crum. (USA)

■**191** Photo used as self promotion for New York photographer Britain Hill. (USA)

■**190** Porträt asiatischer Ordensschwestern, als Eigenwerbung des Photographen Lee Crum verwendet. (USA)

■**191** Als Eigenwerbung verwendete Aufnahme des New Yorker Photographen Britain Hill. (USA)

■**190** Portrait de religieuses asiatiques servant d'autopromotion au photographe Lee Crum. (USA)

■**191** Photo servant d'autopromotion au photographe newyorkais Britain Hill. (USA)

PHOTOGRAPHER:
Lee Crum
CLIENT:
Lee Crum
ART DIRECTOR:
Lee Crum
■**190**

PHOTOGRAPHER:
Britain Hill
CLIENT:
Britain Hill
ART DIRECTOR:
Britain Hill
■191

PHOTOGRAPHER:
Peter Liepke
CLIENT:
Peter Liepke
ART DIRECTOR:
Peter Liepke
■ **192**

■ **192** Portrait of the Indian "Stone King", from a portfolio for photographer Peter Liepke. (USA)

■ **193** Full-page portrait of American author David Leavitt, from an article in *Vogue Italia*. (ITA)

■ **192** Porträt des Indianers «Steinkönig», aus dem Portfolio des Photographen Peter Liepke. (USA)

■ **193** Ganzseitiges Porträt des amerikanischen Schriftstellers David Leavitt, aus einem Beitrag in *Vogue Italia*. (ITA)

■ **192** Portrait de l'Indien «Stone King» (Roi des Pierres), autopromotion du photographe Peter Liepke. (USA)

■ **193** Portrait pleine page de l'écrivain américain David Leavitt pour un article publié dans *Vogue Italia*. (ITA)

PHOTOGRAPHER:
Bolofo
PUBLISHER:
Condé Nast S.p.A.
ART DIRECTOR:
Alberto Nodolini
■193

■**194** Photo by Burkhard von Harder of Hamburg, from an article in the magazine *Photographie* about the Hamburg competition "Flash Art" which is devoted to creative flashlight photography. (SWI)

■**195** For the cover of a brochure of the Houston Boxing Association for the advancement and promotion of this sport. (USA)

■**194** Aufnahme des Hamburger Photographen Burkhard von Harder, aus einem Bericht in *Photographie* über den Hamburger Wettbewerb «Flash Art», der kreativer Blitzlichtphotographie gewidmet ist. (SWI)

■**195** Aufnahme für den Umschlag einer Broschüre der Houston Boxing Association zur Förderung des Boxsports. (USA)

■**194** Photo de Burkhard von Harder, un photographe de Hambourg. Elle est tirée d'un reportage paru dans *Photographie* et consacré à «Flash Art», le concours de la meilleure création photographique au flash de Hambourg. (SWI)

■**195** Photo pour la couverture d'une brochure d'une association en faveur du développement de la boxe à Houston. (USA)

PHOTOGRAPHER:
Burkhard von Harder
PUBLISHER:
Verlag Photographie Ag
ART DIRECTOR:
Peter Wassermann
■**194**

PHOTOGRAPHER:
Don Glentzer

CLIENT:
Houston Boxing
Association

ART DIRECTOR:
Don Glentzer

DESIGNER:
Jackie Dryden

STUDIO:
Glentzer Photography

■195

■**196–200** From a photo book entitled *In the American West*, with portraits by Richard Avedon, published by *Harry N. Abrams*. Shown are: Alfred Lester, dryland farmer, Charboneau, North Dakota, 8/17/82 (*196*); Sandra Bennett, a twelve-year-old from Rocky Ford, Colorado, 8/23/80 (*197*); Boyd Fortin, thirteen-year-old rattlesnake skinner, Sweetwater, Texas, 3/10/79 (*198*); Red Owens, oil field worker, Velma, Oklahoma, 6/12/80 (*190*) and Ronald Fischer, beekeeper, Davis, California, 5/9/81 (*200*). (USA)

■**196–200** Aus einem Photoband mit dem Titel *In the American West* mit Porträts von Richard Avedon, Verlag *Harry N. Abrams*. Hier Alfred Lester, Trockenfarmer, Charboneau, North Dakota, 17.8.82 (*196*); Sandra Bennett, eine Zwölfjährige aus Rocky Ford, Colorado, 23.8.80 (*197*); Boyd Fortin, 13jähriger Klapperschlangenenthäuter, Sweetwater, Texas, 10.3.79 (*198*); Red Owens, Ölfeldarbeiter, Velma, Oklahoma, 12.6.80 (*199*) und Ronald Fischer, Imker, Davis, Kalifornien, 9.5.81 (*200*). (USA)

■**196–200** D'un volume intitulé *In the American West*, publié chez *Harry N. Abrams*, avec des portraits de Richard Avedon. Ici, Alfred Lester, agriculteur, Charboneau, North Dakota, 17.8.82 (*196*); Sandra Bennett, douze ans, Rocky Ford, Colorado, 23.8.80 (*197*); Boyd Fortin, treize ans, Sweetwater, Texas, 10.3.79 (*198*); Red Owens, ouvrier d'un gisement pétrolifère, Velma, Oklahoma, 12.6.80 (*199*) et Ronald Fischer, apiculteur, Davis, Californie, 9.5.81 (*200*). (USA)

PHOTOGRAPHER:
RICHARD AVEDON
PUBLISHER:
HARRY N. ABRAMS
ART DIRECTOR:
MARVIN ISRAEL/
ELIZABETH AVEDON
DESIGNER:
MARVIN ISRAEL/
ELIZABETH AVEDON
■**196–200**

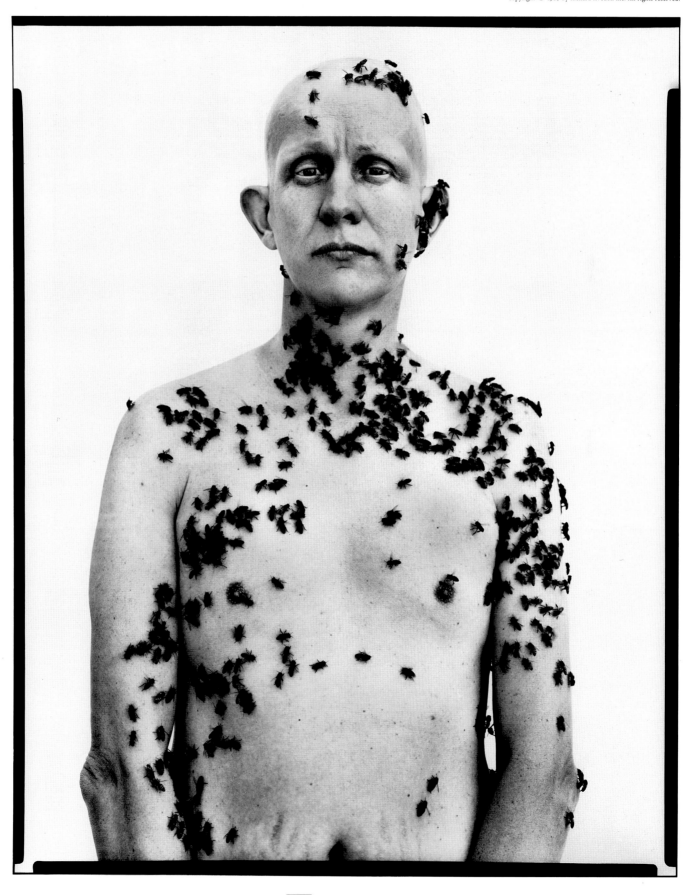

PHOTOGRAPHER:
Philip-Lorca Dicorcia
PUBLISHER:
The Village Voice
Fashion Magazine
ART DIRECTOR:
Yolanda Cuomo
■ **201**

PHOTOGRAPHER:
Amy Arbus
PUBLISHER:
The Village Voice
Fashion Magazine
ART DIRECTOR:
Yolanda Cuomo
■ **202**

■ **201, 202** Photographs from *Vue*, the fashion magazine of the New Yorker weekly magazine *The Village Voice*. *201:* "Men behind bars" – Monty Stilson of the "Spring Lounge"; *202:* From an article about tattooing entitled "Flesh and Ink". (USA)

■ **201, 202** Aufnahmen aus *Vue*, dem Modemagazin der New Yorker Wochenzeitung *The Village Voice*. *201:* »Barkeeper tragen Streifen«, hier Monty Stilson von der »Spring Lounge«; *202:* Aus einem Beitrag über das Tätowieren. (USA)

■ **201, 202** Photos de *Vue*, le magazine de modes paraissant dans l'hebdomadaire *The Village Voice*. *201:* «Les barmen portent des rayures»; ici, Monty Stilson du «Spring Lounge.» *202:* d'un article sur les tatouages. (USA)

PHOTOGRAPHER:
Bill White
CLIENT:
Bill White Studio
ART DIRECTOR:
Bill White
■ 203

PHOTOGRAPHER:
Eileen Cowin
PUBLISHER:
Los Angeles County
Museum of Art
DESIGNER:
Deenie Yudell/Sandy Bell
■ **204**

■ **203** Photograph for self-promotional purposes for Bill White of New York. (USA)

■ **204** Photograph by Eileen Cowin which was presented in a catalog issued by the Los Angeles County Museum of Art under the title *New American Photography*. (USA)

■ **203** Als Eigenwerbung des Photographen Bill White, New York, verwendete Aufnahme. (USA)

■ **204** Aufnahme der Photographin Eileen Cowin, die in einem Katalog des Los Angeles County Museum of Art mit dem Titel *New American Photography* vorgestellt wird. (USA)

■ **203** Photo utilisée comme autopromotion par le photographe newyorkais Bill White. (USA)

■ **204** Photo d'Eileen Cowin: cette photographe est présentée dans un catalogue du Los Angeles County Museum of Art intitulé *New American Photography*. (USA)

PHOTOGRAPHER:
Neal Slavin

PUBLISHER:
*André Deutsch/
Aperture Books*

ART DIRECTOR:
*Peter Harrison/
Susan Hochbaum*

DESIGNER:
Pentagram Design

■ **205–210**

PHOTOGRAPHER:
Hans Neleman

PUBLISHER:
Anthony Russell, Inc.

ART DIRECTOR:
Anthony Russell

DESIGNER:
Casey Clark

AGENCY:
Anthony Russell, Inc.

■ **211, 212**

■ **211, 212** Photos from an article about photographer Hans Neleman in *U.S. Eye*. Shown here is photographer Duane Michaels in his apartment (*211*) and New York artist Mark Lambrechts (*212*) (this photograph was commissioned by the French art magazine *Mots de Passe*). (USA)

■ **211, 212** Aufnahmen aus einem Beitrag über den Photographen Hans Neleman in *U.S. Eye*. Hier der Photograph Duane Michaels in seiner Wohnung (*211*) und der in New York lebende Künstler Mark Lambrechts (*212*) (die Aufnahme entstand im Auftrag der französischen Kunstzeitschrift *Mots de Passe*). (USA)

■ **211, 212** Photos d'un article sur le photographe Hans Neleman paru dans *U.S. Eye*. Ici, le photographe Duane Michaels dans son appartement (*211*) et l'artiste Mark Lambrechts, établi à New York (*212*) (la photo a été réalisée pour la revue d'art française *Mots de Passe*). (USA)

ANIMALS / TIERE / ANIMAUX

PHOTOGRAPHER:
Stak Aivaliotis

CLIENT:
Interface

ART DIRECTOR:
Gary Betts

AGENCY:
Doyle Dane Bernbach

■ 213

PHOTOGRAPHER:
Stak Aivaliotis

CLIENT:
S.D. Warren Paper Co.

ART DIRECTOR:
Cheryl Heller

DESIGNER:
Cheryl Heller

AGENCY:
HBM/Creamer Design Group
■ 214

■ **213** "Carpet tiles for people who would never be seen with carpet tiles." Photograph from an advertisement for carpet tiles by *Interface.* (GBR)

■ **214** "Coating...makes the sheet, just as surely as it makes the sheep." Sheepskin in comparison with a paper by *S.D. Warren;* photo for an advertisement on this theme. (USA)

■ **213** Aufnahme aus einer Anzeige für Teppichfliesen von *Interface.* Hier soll bewiesen werden, wie perfekt sich selbst Muster verlegen lassen. (GBR)

■ **214** Die Eigenschaften des Schaffells verglichen mit denen einer Papierqualität von *S.D. Warren* sind Gegenstand der Anzeige, zu der diese Aufnahme gehört. (USA)

■ **213** Photo pour une annonce de plaques de moquette *Interface* qui entend démontrer que même des motifs bigarrés peuvent se composer sans problème. (GBR)

■ **214** Les qualités d'une peau de mouton comparées à celles d'une qualité de papier *S.D. Warren*, voilà le sujet d'une annonce illustrée par cette photo. (USA)

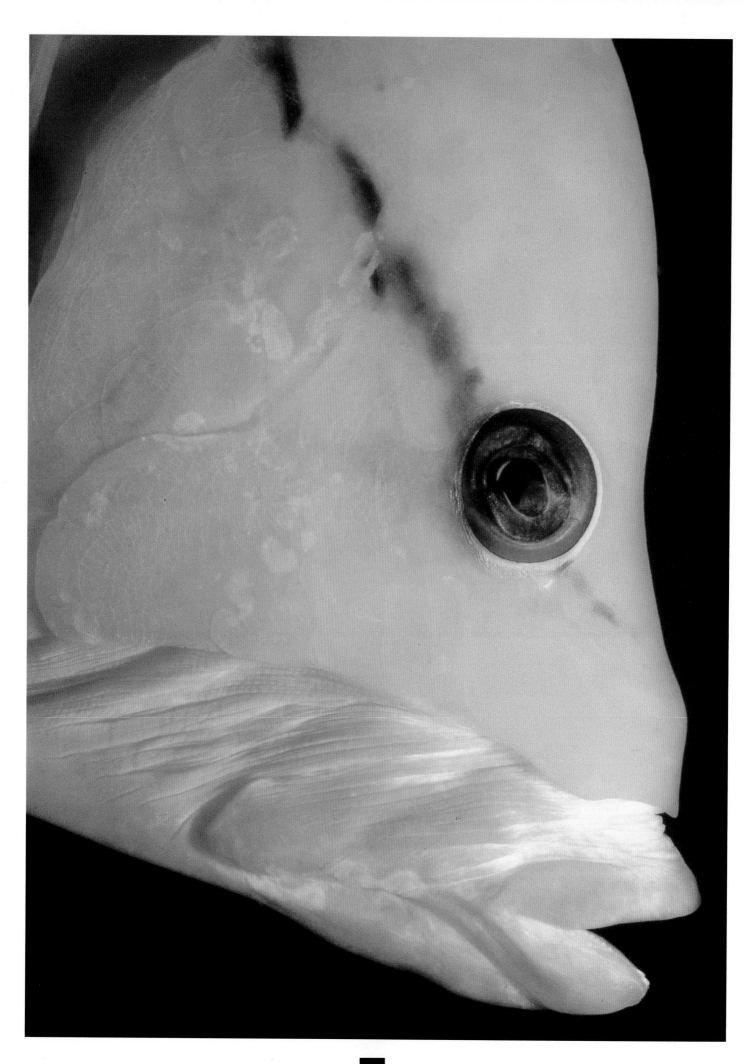

PHOTOGRAPHER:
Jeff Rotman
PUBLISHER:
Minolta Camera Co. Ltd.
ART DIRECTOR:
Fred O. Bechlen
■ **215–217**

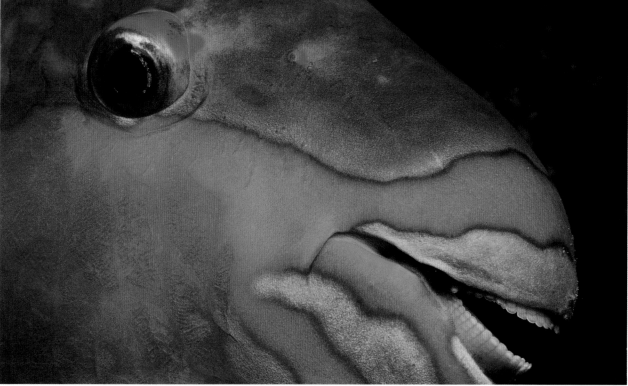

■ **215–217** Photographs from an interview in the *Minolta Mirror* with Jeff Rotman, a specialist in underwater photography. *215* shows the profile of a butterfish by night, *216* soft corals feeding at night, and *217* a parrotfish dozing. All photographs were taken in the Red Sea. (JPN)

■ **215–217** Aufnahmen aus einem Interview mit dem auf Unterwasserphotographie spezialisierten Photographen Jeff Rotman in *Minolta Mirror*. *215* zeigt das nächtliche Profil eines Butterfisches, *216* Korallen und *217* einen dösenden Seepapageien. Alle Aufnahmen stammen aus dem Roten Meer. (JPN)

■ **215–217** Photos illustrant une interview avec le photographe sous-marin Jeff Rotman, dans *Minolta Mirror*. La photo *215* montre le profil nocturne d'une gonelle commune, *216* des coreaux, et *217* un poisson-perroquet surpris en train de rêvasser. Toutes ces photos ont été réalisées dans la mer Rouge. (JPN)

PHOTOGRAPHER:
Michael Fodgen

PUBLISHER:
Gruner + Jahr Ag & Co.

ART DIRECTOR:
Erwin Ehret

■ **218, 219**

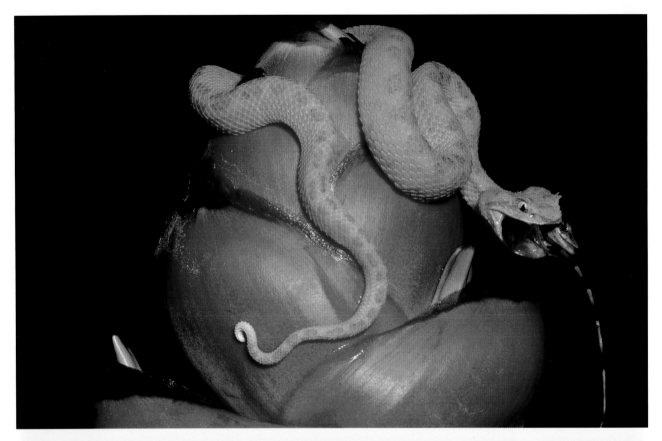

PHOTOGRAPHER:
Li Xin
PUBLISHER:
CAAC Beijing
ART DIRECTOR:
Kan Tai-keung
DESIGNER:
Kan Tai-keung/Freeman Lau
AGENCY:
SS Design & Production
■ **220**

■ **218, 219** "Big Mouth and Poison Tooth" is the title of the feature in *Geo* to which these double-spread photos belong. Here an Eyelash Viper (*218*), a tree snake of which there are varieties in six different colorations, and a Parrot Snake (*219*), famous for their camouflage. (GER)

■ **220** Photo for the cover of *Peng Cheng*, the inflight magazine for passengers of the *CAAC Beijing* airline. (HKG)

■ **218, 219** «Grossmaul und Giftzahn» ist der Titel des Beitrags in *Geo*, zu dem diese doppelseitigen Aufnahmen gehören. Hier eine Schlegel-Lanzenotter (*218*), eine Baumschlange, die es in einem halben Dutzend unterschiedlichen Farbtönen gibt, und eine Schlanknatter (*219*). (GER)

■ **220** Aufnahme für den Umschlag von *Peng Cheng*, Passagier-Zeitschrift der Fluggesellschaft *CAAC Beijing*. (HKG)

■ **218, 219** «Grande gueule et crochet à venin», voilà le titre d'un article de *Geo* illustré de ces photos double page. On y voit la vipère «Schlegel» (*218*), un serpent d'arbre dont il existe une demi-douzaine de variétés étincelant dans des coloris différents, et une vipère perroquet (*219*). (GER)

■ **220** Photo de couverture de *Peng Cheng*, magazine pour les passagers de la compagnie aérienne *CAAC Beijing*. (HKG)

■ **221** A truffle seeker with his pig; double-spread photo from an article about the (French) Dordogne region; in *Merian*. (GER)

■ **221** Ein Trüffelsucher mit seinem Schwein; doppelseitige Aufnahme aus einem Bericht über die Dordogne, in *Merian*. (GER)

■ **221** Un trufficulteur avec son porc; photo double page pour un article que le magazine *Merian* consacre à la Dordogne. (GER)

PHOTOGRAPHER:
Bruno Barbey/Magnum
PUBLISHER:
Hoffmann & Campe
ART DIRECTOR:
Erika Schmied
■ **221**

PHOTOGRAPHER:
Alain Ernoult

PUBLISHER:
Publications Filipacchi

ART DIRECTOR:
Eric Colmet Daage

■ **222**

■ **222** Photograph from the cockpit of an Alpha jet of the French airforce, taken to mark the occasion of a visit of this famous French "Patrouille" to the centenary celebrations of the Statue of Liberty in the USA. Alain Ernoult used a fisheye lens 1/1000 s., with *Kodachrome 64 Pro.* (FRA)

■ **223** Photograph of a *Concorde* flying over the luxury liner Queen Elizabeth 2, escorted by a crack formation-flying squadron of the Royal Air Force. From a feature in *Stern* about this controversial plane that has been in service for ten years. (GER)

■ **222** Aufnahme aus dem Cockpit eines Alpha-Jets der französischen Luftwaffe, entstanden anlässlich eines Besuches dieser berühmten französischen »Patrouille« zur Hundertjahres-Feier der Freiheitsstatue in den USA. Alain Ernoult benutzte ein Fisheye-Objektiv 1/1000 s., mit *Kodachrome 64 Pro.* (FRA)

■ **223** Aufnahme einer *Concorde*, die, eskortiert von der Kunstflugstaffel der Royal Air Force, den Luxusliner »Queen Elizabeth 2« passiert. Aus einem Beitrag im *Stern* über dieses umstrittene Zivilflugzeug, das seit zehn Jahren im Einsatz ist. (GER)

■ **222** Photo prise à partir du cockpit d'un Alpha-Jet de l'armée de l'air française, à l'occasion d'un vol de la fameuse »Patrouille de France« lors de la fête du centenaire de la statue de la Liberté aux USA. Alain Ernoult a utilisé un objectif »fish eye« 1/1000 s. et un *Kodachrome 64 Pro.* (FRA)

■ **223** Photo d'un *Concorde* qui, escorté de l'escadrille d'acrobatie aérienne de la Royal Air Force, passe au-dessus du luxueux »Queen Elizabeth 2«. D'un article paru dans *Stern* sur cet avion controversé, en service depuis dix ans. (GER)

PHOTOGRAPHER:
Arthur Gibson
PUBLISHER:
Gruner + Jahr
ART DIRECTOR:
Wolfgang Behnken
■ **223**

PHOTOGRAPHER:
Clint Clemens

CLIENT:
S. D. Warren Paper Co.

ART DIRECTOR:
Cheryl Heller

DESIGNER:
Cheryl Heller

AGENCY:
HBM/Creamer
Design Group

■ **224–227**

■ **224–227** Photographs from "Runability" - an advertising brochure for the paper producers *S.D. Warren*. Using classics of the American auto industry the firm demonstrates the quality of its paper. *224* shows a *Thunderbird*, *225* and *226* a *Cadillac*, *227* a *Buick*. (USA)

■ **224–227** Aufnahmen aus einer Werbebroschüre für den Papierhersteller *S.D. Warren*, der anhand dieser Klassiker der amerikanischen Autoindustrie die Qualität seines Papiers unter Beweis stellen will. *224* zeigt einen *Thunderbird*, *225* und *226* einen *Cadillac*, *227* einen *Buick*. (USA)

■ **224–227** Photos d'une brochure publicitaire du fabricant de papier *S.D. Warren* qui veut, au moyen de ces classiques de l'industrie automobile américaine, prouver la qualité de son papier. La photo *224* montre une *Thunderbird*, *225* et *226* une *Cadillac*, *227* une *Buick*. (USA)

PHOTOGRAPHER:
*Dingo/Photo
Agence Vandystadt/
Focus*

PUBLISHER:
Hoffmann & Campe

ART DIRECTOR:
Hartmut Brückner

■ 228

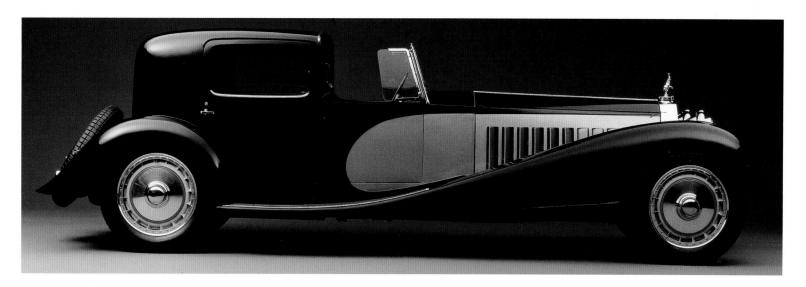

PHOTOGRAPHER:
Peter Forster

PUBLISHER:
Hoffmann & Campe

CLIENT:
Badische Tabakmanufaktur
Roth-Händle GmbH & Co.

ART DIRECTOR:
Hartmut Brückner

■ **229**

■ **228, 229** Photograph of a *Jaguar* for the cover of the monthly magazine *Merian* and a *Bugatti Royale* Type 41 built 1931, shown inside on a double spread with folding flaps. This is a special issue of the magazine to mark the centenary of the automobile. (GER)

■ **228, 229** Aufnahmen eines *Jaguars* für den Umschlag des Monatsheftes *Merian* und eines *Bugatti Royale* Typ 41, Baujahr 1931, der auf einer Doppelseite mit Auslegern im Inhalt gezeigt wird. Es handelt sich um ein Sonderheft zum 100. Geburtstag des Automobils. (GER)

■ **228, 229** Photo d'une *Jaguar*, parue en couverture du mensuel *Merian*, et une *Bugatti Royale* Type 41, datant de 1931, qui figure sur une double page à rabats à l'intérieur du magazine. Il s'agit d'un numéro spécial pour le 100e anniversaire de l'automobile. (GER)

PHOTOGRAPHER:
Stephen Salmieri

PUBLISHER:
Rizzoli

ART DIRECTOR:
*Walter Bernard/
Milton Glaser*

DESIGNER:
*Walter Bernard/
Milton Glaser*

AGENCY:
WBMG, Inc.

■ **230**

PHOTOGRAPHER:
Joe Baraban

CLIENT:
Joe Baraban

DESIGNER:
John Heck

AGENCY:
Herring Design

■ **231**

■ **230** For the dust jacket of a book entitled *Cadillac*. The book contains hand colored black-and-white photographs by Stephen Salmieri who, with the help of *Cadillac*, offers a portrait of the United States. (USA)

■ **231** Photograph of a *Cadillac* for an invitation in poster form to celebrate the birthdays of photographer Joe Baraban and his wife Perry. (USA)

■ **230** Für den Schutzumschlag eines Buches mit dem Titel *Cadillac* verwendete Aufnahme. Das Buch enthält handkolorierte Schwarzweissaufnahmen des Photographen Stephen Salmieri, der mit Hilfe des *Cadillacs* ein Porträt der USA zeichnete. (USA)

■ **231** Aufnahme eines *Cadillacs* für eine im Plakatformat gestaltete Einladung zur Feier von runden Geburtstagen des Photographen Joe Baraban und seiner Frau Perry. (USA)

■ **230** Photo reproduite en couverture d'un livre intitulé *Cadillac*, qui contient des photos noir et blanc, coloriées à la main, du photographe Stephen Salmieri. Celui-ci, à l'aide d'une *Cadillac*, trace un portrait des Etats-Unis. (USA)

■ **231** Photo d'une *Cadillac* pour une invitation, conçue comme affiche, pour la fête organisée à l'occasion de l'anniversaire du photographe Joe Baraban et de sa femme Perry. (USA)

PHOTOGRAPHER:
Dietmar Henneka

CLIENT:
Porsche

ART DIRECTOR:
Günther Tibi

AGENCY:
Wensauer & Partner

■ **232–235**

■ **232–235** Photographs from an advertising campaign for *Porsche* under the slogan "*Porsche*, driving in its most beautiful form." Some of the selling points: "7 years longterm guarantee against rusting through" (*232*); "A special amount of active and passive safety" (*234*); "The new *Porsche 969* can be considered as the aim for the ultimate car" (*235*). (GER)

■ **232–235** Aufnahmen aus einer Werbekampagne für *Porsche* unter dem Motto «*Porsche*, Fahren in seiner schönsten Form». Einige der Argumente: «7 Jahre Langzeitgarantie gegen Durchrosten» (*232*); «Ein besonderes Mass an aktiver und passiver Sicherheit» (*234*); «Der neue *Porsche 969* ist als das Streben nach dem optimalen Auto zu verstehen» (*235*). (GER)

■ **232–235** Photos d'une campagne de publicité pour *Porsche*, basée sur le slogan: «*Porsche*, rouler dans sa meilleur forme». Quelques-uns des arguments: «7 ans de garantie contre la rouille» (*232*); «Une certaine dose de sécurité active et passive» (*234*); «La nouvelle *Porsche 969* doit être considerée comme une aspiration à la perfection» (*235*). (GER)

PHOTOGRAPHER:
Dietmar Henneka

PUBLISHER:
Dietmar Henneka

ART DIRECTOR:
Urs Schwerzmann/
Hanspeter Kamm

DESIGNER:
Ute Vollenweider

AGENCY:
Büro Schwerzmann
■ **236**

■ **236** Photo from a large-size image magazine bearing the title *Auss-Puff* (Exhaust) for photographer Dietmar Henneka. (GER)

■ **237** "*Kodak* pours on the color." Photograph from a promotion campaign for a new film by *Kodak*. (USA)

■ **238** From an advertising campaign for *Honda* scooters. (USA)

■ **236** Aus einem grossformatigen Image-Magazin mit dem Titel *Auss-Puff*, für den Photographen Dietmar Henneka. (GER)

■ **237** «*Kodak* giesst die Farbe drüber.» Aufnahme aus einer Werbekampagne für einen neuen Film von *Kodak*. (USA)

■ **238** Aus einer Werbekampagne für *Honda*-Motorroller. (USA)

■ **236** Photo d'un magazine de prestige grand format intitulé *Auss-Puff*, pour le photographe Dietmar Henneka. (GER)

■ **237** «*Kodak* verse la couleur dessus.» Photo d'une campagne de publicité pour une nouvelle pellicule de *Kodak*. (USA)

■ **238** D'une campagne pour les scooters *Honda*. (USA)

PHOTOGRAPHER:
Clint Clemens

CLIENT:
Eastman Kodak Co.

ART DIRECTOR:
Kai Mui

AGENCY:
Rumrill-Hoyt

■ 237

PHOTOGRAPHER:
Joe Baraban

CLIENT:
Honda Scooters

ART DIRECTOR:
Susan Hoffman

AGENCY:
Wieden, Kennedy

■ 238

■ **239** Example of the photographs appearing in a hanging calendar for hi-fi loudspeakers made by *quadral*. (GER)

■ **239** Beispiel der Aufnahmen aus einem Wandkalender für Hifi-Lautsprecher der Marke *quadral*. (GER)

■ **239** Exemple de photos d'un calendrier mural pour les enceintes haut fidélité de la marque *quadral*. (GER)

PHOTOGRAPHER:
Gunter Sachs
CLIENT:
All-Akustik
ART DIRECTOR:
Heinz Huke
AGENCY:
GD Graphic & Design OHG
■**239**

PHOTOGRAPHER:
ROBERT LLEWELLYN
PUBLISHER:
FORT CHURCH PUBLISHERS, INC.
ART DIRECTOR:
JAMES B. PATRICK
DESIGNER:
DONALD G. PAULHUS
■ **241**

■ **241** From a book of photographs about the University of Pennsylvania for which Robert Llewellyn took a total of 2000 shots. The book is devised for students. (USA)

■ **242** Surfer on the beach at Biarritz. Photo from a feature in *Merian* about the Basque coast. (GER)

■ **241** Aufnahme aus einem Bildband über die University of Pennsylvania, für den Robert Llewellyn insgesamt 2000 Photos machte. Das Buch ist für die Studenten bestimmt. (USA)

■ **242** Surfer am Strand von Biarritz. Aufnahme aus einem Beitrag über die baskische Küste, in *Merian*. (GER)

■ **241** L'une des 2000 photos dont Robert Llewellyn a illustré un album consacré à l'Université de Pennsylvanie et qui est destiné au corps estudiantin. (USA)

■ **242** Un surfeur sur la plage de Biarritz. Photo pour un article du magazine *Merian* qui traite de la côte basque. (GER)

PHOTOGRAPHER:
Pierre Gascogne/
Agence Vandystadt

PUBLISHER:
Hoffmann & Campe

ART DIRECTOR:
Erika Schmied

■ 242

PHOTOGRAPHER:
Harald Sund

CLIENT:
Champion International Corp.

ART DIRECTOR:
Thomas D. Morin

DESIGNER:
Thomas D. Morin

AGENCY:
Jack Hough Associates, Inc.

■ **243–248**

■ **243–248** Photographs from a brochure issued by the paper producers *Champion* and devoted to a husky race in Alaska. *243-246* show "Rainy Pass" on which in cold weather there is a danger of storms, while at higher temperatures there is a threat of avalanches. (USA)

■ **243–248** Aufnahmen aus einer Broschüre des Papierherstellers *Champion*, die einem Schlittenhund-Rennen in Alaska gewidmet ist. *243-246* zeigen den «Rainy Pass» (Regenpass), auf dem bei Kälte die Gefahr von Sturm, bei höheren Temperaturen wiederum Lawinen drohen. (USA)

■ **243–248** Photos illustrant une brochure du groupe papetier *Champion* sur les courses de chiens de traîneaux en Alaska. *243-246:* le col des pluies (Rainy Pass), dangereux en raison des tempêtes qui y sévissent par grand froid et des avalanches qu'y déclenche toute remontée de la température. (USA)

PHOTOGRAPHER:
Guy Sauvage/
Agence Vandystadt
PUBLISHER:
Sport Net, Inc.
ART DIRECTOR:
Dave Nanni
DESIGNER:
Dave Nanni/Reena Brown
AGENCY:
Graphis, Inc.
■ **249**

■ **249** From a brochure for *Sport Net*, a sports and holiday club, which here gives information about parachuting. (USA)

■ **250** Photo used in the annual report of a bank. (USA)

■ **249** Aus einer Broschüre für *Sport Net*, einen Sport-Ferien-Club, der hier über das Fallschirmspringen informiert. (USA)

■ **250** Aufnahme für den Jahresbericht einer Bank. (USA)

■ **249** Pour une brochure de *Sport Net*, un club de vacances sportives qui renseigne ici sur ses cours de parachutisme. (USA)

■ **250** Photo utilisée pour le rapport annuel d'une banque. (USA)

PHOTOGRAPHER:
Peter Jones
CLIENT:
Indian Head Bank
DESIGNER:
Dennis Russo
AGENCY:
William Wondriska Associates
■ **250**

PHOTOGRAPHER:
Maria Mühlberger
PUBLISHER:
Gruner + Jahr AG & Co.
ART DIRECTOR:
Thomas Höpker
■ **251**

■ **251** Photo from a reportage in the magazine *Stern* on a book on sports photography (*Der Traum vom Sieg – Kampf und Kult in der Sportphotografie*) published by *Gruner + Jahr*. The photographer Maria Mühlberger symbolizes the courage of the lone contender who never gives up in her shot of a mud-bespattered cross-country cyclist. (GER)

■ **251** Aus einer Reportage im Magazin *Stern* über das Buch von Matthias Matussek und Christiane Gehner: *Der Traum vom Sieg – Kampf und Kult in der Sportfotografie*, erschienen im Verlag *Gruner + Jahr*. Die Photographin Maria Mühlberger lässt mit dem schlammbespritzten Querfeldeinfahrer die alte Tugend des Einzelkämpfers triumphieren, der nicht aufgibt. (GER)

■ **251** D'un reportage du magazine *Stern* sur le livre de Matthias Matussek et Christiane Gehner: «Le rêve de la victoire – Lutte et culte dans la photographie de sport», paru aux éditions *Gruner + Jahr*. La photographie de Maria Mühlberger de ce coureur de cyclocross couvert de boue consacre les valeurs traditionnelles de combat individuel. (GER)

PHOTOGRAPHER:
Robert van der Hilst
PUBLISHER:
Marie Claire
ART DIRECTOR:
Walter Rospert
■ **252–259**

■ **260** From an article: "Runaway Kids" first published in *Life* and appearing in *Zeitmagazin* about street children in Seattle. Shown, a sixteen and a seventeen-year-old with a Colt 45. (USA)

■ **261** From an article in *Tempo* about "Soldiers of Fortune", a group of weapon fanatics, mercenaries from Nicaragua, Vietnam veterans and young adventurers in the USA. (USA)

■ **260** Aufnahme aus einer von *Life* übernommenen Reportage im *Zeitmagazin* über Strassenkinder in Seattle. Hier ein Sechzehn- und ein Siebzehnjähriger mit einem 45er Colt. (USA)

■ **261** Aus einer Reportage in *Tempo* über «Soldiers of Fortune», eine Gruppe von Waffennarren, Söldnern aus Nicaragua, Vietnam-Veteranen und jungen Abenteurern in den USA. (USA)

■ **260** Photo d'un reportage de *Life* repris par le *Zeitmagazin*, consacré aux enfants des rues de Seattle: deux adolescents de 16 et 17 ans en possession d'un Colt 45. (USA)

■ **261** «Soldiers of fortune» aux Etats-Unis, recrutés parmi les enragés de la gâchette, les mercenaires du Nicaragua, les vétérans du Viêt-nam et des jeunes aventuriers. Paru dans *Tempo*. (USA)

PHOTOGRAPHER:
Mary Ellen Mark
PUBLISHER:
Zeitverlag
Gerd Bucerius KG
ART DIRECTOR:
Christian Diener
■ **260**

PHOTOGRAPHER:
Bob Wagner
PUBLISHER:
Jahreszeiten-Verlag GmbH
ART DIRECTOR:
Lo Breier/Ecke Bonk
DESIGNER:
Judith Grubinger/Dirk Linke
■ 261

PHOTOGRAPHER:
Yan Morvan/Sipa Press
PUBLISHER:
Gruner + Jahr Ag & Co.
ART DIRECTOR:
Erwin Ehret
■ **262**

PHOTOGRAPHER:
Michael Coyne

PUBLISHER:
Gruner + Jahr AG & Co.

ART DIRECTOR:
Erwin Ehret

■ **263**

■ **262** Double-spread photograph from an article about the situation in Beirut, appearing in *Geo*. Shown is a captain of the Shiite Amal militia with his family. He was a trainer of kamikaze commandos. The woman in the framed photograph blew herself up at an Israeli checkpoint in a car packed full of dynamite. (GER)

■ **263** "The desire of suffering as a mark of virtue and readiness of die in war" is the title of this shot from an editorial feature about Iran, appearing in *Geo*. (GER)

■ **262** Aufnahme aus einem Artikel über die Lage in Beirut, erschienen in *Geo*. Hier ein Hauptmann der schiitischen Amal-Miliz mit seiner Familie. Er trainiert Kamikaze-Kommandos – die Frau auf dem gerahmten Photo hat sich mit einem Auto voll Dynamit an einem israelischen Checkpoint in die Luft gesprengt. (GER)

■ **263** «Die Lust am Leid als Zeichen der Tugend und Opferbereitschaft im Krieg» ist der Titel zu dieser Aufnahme aus einem redaktionellen Beitrag über den Iran in *Geo*. (GER)

■ **262** Pour un article de *Geo* relatant la situation qui prévaut à Beyrouth. Ici un capitaine de la milice chi'ite Amal avec sa famille. Il entraîne des commandos de kamikazes. La femme qui figure sur la photo encadrée est ainsi allée à la mort en conduisant une voiture bourrée de dynamite jusqu'à un poste militaire israélien. (GER)

■ **263** «L'acceptation joyeuse de la souffrance: signe de vertu et d'esprit de sacrifice en temps de guerre», voilà la légende de cette photo qui illustre un article de *Geo* sur l'Iran. (GER)

PHOTOGRAPHER:
Fred Prase
PUBLISHER:
Unionsverlag/
Hoffmann & Campe
■ **264–271**

■ **264–271** Photographs by police superintendent Fred Prase taken from a book entitled "Fire Pond" (*Feuerteich*, Unionsverlag, Zürich) about Frankfurt's railway-station area. (They were also shown in an issue of *Merian* dedicated to Frankfurt.) *264*: the daily work of a police officer; *265*: Goethe anniversary year – even for the police, and an Indian who was found completely naked; *266*: foreigners account for 80% of the population in the railway area; *267*: death of a traveller in the main station; *268*: a woman in the police station, still under shock after having been locked in a lift; *269*: US soldiers after receiving their pay; *270*: a body in the service room of the S railway station; *271*: death without mourning – two employees of the municipal mortuary. (GER)

■ **264–271** Aufnahmen des Polizei-Hauptkommissars Fred Prase aus einem Buch mit dem Titel *Feuerteich* (Unionsverlag, Zürich) über das Frankfurter Bahnhofsviertel. (Sie wurden ebenfalls in einem *Merian*-Heft über Frankfurt verwendet.) *264*: Die tägliche Arbeit eines Polizeibeamten; *265*: Goethejahr auch im Polizeirevier, und ein Inder, der völlig unbekleidet aufgefunden wurde; *266*: Ausländer stellen 80% der Bevölkerung des Bahnhofsviertels; *267*: Tod eines Reisenden im Hauptbahnhof; *268*: eine Frau, die in einem Fahrstuhl eingeschlossen war, und ihre Reaktion in der Revierzelle der Polizei; *269*: US-Soldaten nach der Auszahlung ihres Solds; *270*: ein Toter im Dienstraum eines S-Bahnhofs; *271*: Tod ohne Trauer: die städtischen Leichenträger. (GER)

■ **264–271** Photos du commissaire principal Fred Prase tirées d'un livre intitulé «L'etang de feu» (*Feuerteich*, Unionsverlag, Zurich) dans le quartier de la gare de Francfort. (Reprises aussi dans un numéro de *Merian* sur Francfort.) *264*: le travail quotidien d'un policier; *265*: célébration de l'année commémorative de Goethe au commissariat, et un Indien trouvé complètement nu; *266*: les étrangers constituent de 80% de la population du quartier; *267*: mort d'un voyageur à la gare centrale; *268*: une femme restée enfermée dans un ascenseur: sa réaction une fois libérée et amenée au commissariat; *269*: soldats américains le jour de paie; *270*: cadavre dans les locaux de service d'une station de métro; *271*: la mort sans deuil: deux croque-morts municipaux. (GER)

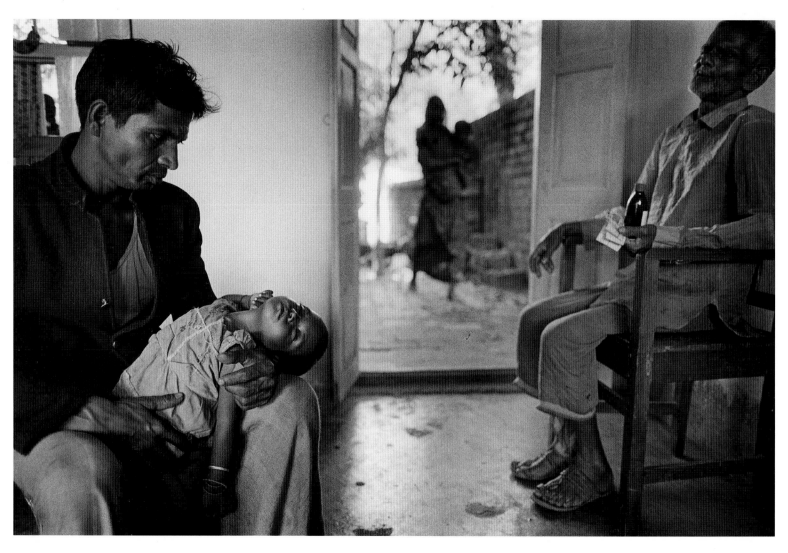

PHOTOGRAPHER:
Mary Ellen Mark
PUBLISHER:
Asmp
Friends of Photography
ART DIRECTOR:
Ulrich Ruchti
DESIGNER:
Ulrich Ruchti
AGENCY:
RF&R Design
■272

PHOTOGRAPHER:
Janet Knott
PUBLISHER:
The Boston Globe
ART DIRECTOR:
Ronn Campisi
DESIGNER:
Ronn Campisi
■273

■**272** Photo from a book published by *Friends of Photography: Mother Teresa and her Missions in Calcutta.* (USA)

■**273** Photograph from an article in *The Boston Globe:* "We are helping people live till they die" - relating to Aids patients. (USA)

■**272** Aus einem bei *Friends of Photography* erschienenen Buch: »Mutter Teresa und ihre Missionen in Kalkutta.« (USA)

■**273** Aufnahme aus einem Artikel in *The Boston Globe* über eine spezielle Betreuung von Aids-Patienten in Boston. (USA)

■**272** D'un livre paru chez *Friends of Photography:* »Mère Teresa et ses missions de Calcutta«. (USA)

■**273** Photo d'un article du *Boston Globe* sur une association qui offre un réconfort moral aux malades du Sida. (USA)

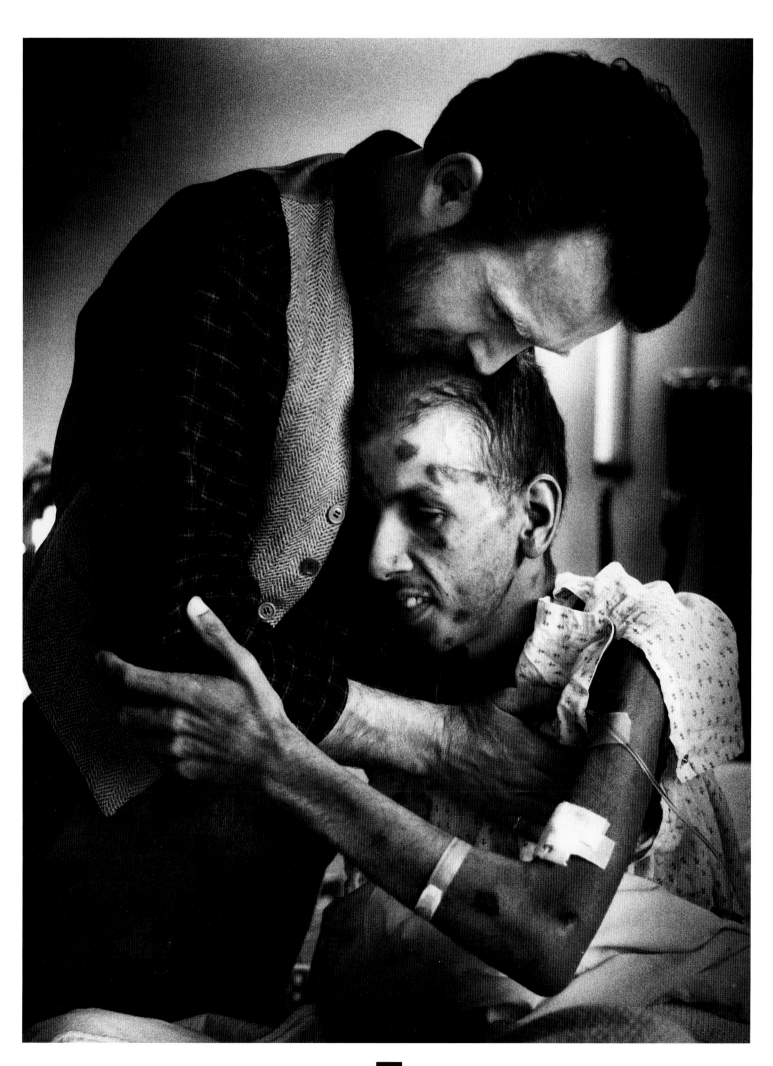

PHOTOGRAPHER:
Sebastião Salgado/
Magnum
PUBLISHER:
Publications Filipacchi
ART DIRECTOR:
Eric Colmet Daage
■ **274**

■ **274** Walking through the dried out Lake Faguibin in the region of Gondam, groups of Nomads leaving the district for the towns where there might be food and shelter. One of the pictures from the Sahel, shot by Sebastião Salgado, in the hope that mankind's conscience would be stirred. Published in *Photo*, the series of photos is on exhibit in France for two years, and later will be shown abroad. (FRA)

■ **274** Gruppen von Nomaden aus Mali beim Durchqueren des ausgetrockneten Sees Faguibin, auf der Suche nach Orten, wo sie Nahrung und Unterkunft finden. Eine der Aufnahmen, die Sebastião Salgado in der Sahelzone machte, in der Hoffnung, das Gewissen der Menschheit aufzurütteln. Sie wurden in *Photo* veröffentlicht und sind während zweier Jahre in Ausstellungen in Frankreich und danach im Ausland zu sehen. (FRA)

■ **274** Mali, région de lac Faguibin – ces nomades marchent vers la périphérie des villes dans l'espoir de trouver arbri et nourriture. Une des photos ramenées du Sahel par Sebastão Salgado dans l'espoir de réveiller la consience des nantis. Publiée dans *Photo*, où elle illustre un reportage, la série fera l'objet d'expositions organisées en France durant deux ans, puis à l'étranger (Londres, Amsterdam, Lausanne, New York).(FRA)

STILL LIFE / STILLEBEN / NATURE MORTE

PHOTOGRAPHER:
Ed Carey

CLIENT:
Ed Carey

ART DIRECTOR:
Ed Carey

DESIGNER:
Jorgensen Design

STUDIO:
Ed Carey
■276

PHOTOGRAPHER:
Hank Benson

CLIENT:
Balzer/Shopes

ART DIRECTOR:
Michael Osborne

DESIGNER:
Michael Osborne

AGENCY:
Michael Osborne Design, Inc.
◀■275

■**275** Photograph from a calendar for the printers *Balzer/Shopes* to demonstrate their know-how in the reproduction of "the most delicate color combinations." (USA)

■**276** Photograph used in a self-promotion calendar by the photographer Ed Carey. (USA)

■**275** Aufnahme aus einem Kalender für die Druckerei *Balzer/ Shopes*, die hier ihr Können in der Wiedergabe der «delikatesten Farbzusammenstellungen» demonstrieren will. (USA)

■**276** Für einen Eigenwerbungs-Kalender des Photographen Ed Carey verwendete Aufnahme. (USA)

■**275** Photo illustrant un calendrier de l'imprimerie *Balzer/Sho- pes*, qui entend démontrer ainsi son savoir-faire en matière de «combinaisons de couleurs particulièrement délicates». (USA)

■**276** Photo utilisée pour un calendrier autopromotionnel du photographe Ed Carey. (USA)

PHOTOGRAPHER:
Terry Heffernan
CLIENT:
Utilicorp United Inc.
DESIGNER:
Mark Sackett
AGENCY:
John Muller
■ **277, 278**

■ **277, 278** Full-page photos from an annual report of UtiliCorp United Inc., an electric and natural gas utility company. (USA)

■ **279, 280** Photographs for the advertising brochure of a printers. *279* was used for the cover. (USA)

■ **277, 278** Ganzseitige Aufnahmen aus einem Jahresbericht der UtiliCorp United Inc., eines Gas- und Elektrizitätswerks. (USA)

■ **279, 280** Aufnahmen für die Werbebroschüre einer Druckerei. *279* wurde für den Umschlag verwendet. (USA)

■ **277, 278** Photos pleine page pour un rapport annuel de l'UtiliCorp United Inc., producteur de gaz et d'éléctricité. (USA)

■ **279, 280** Photos pour la brochure publicitaire d'un imprimeur. *279* a été utilisée pour la couverture. (USA)

PHOTOGRAPHER:
Jim Sims

CLIENT:
Printing Resources, Inc.

ART DIRECTOR:
Steven Sessions

DESIGNER:
Steven Sessions

AGENCY:
Steven Sessions, Inc.

■ **279, 280**

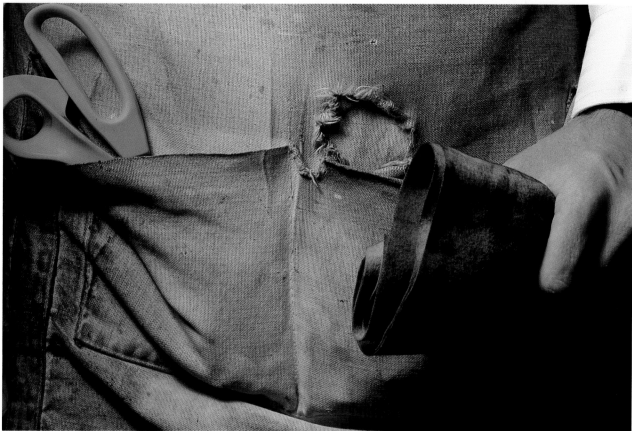

PHOTOGRAPHER:
Klaus Ohlenforst
CLIENT:
Robbe & Berking
ART DIRECTOR:
Werner Würdinger
DESIGNER:
Werner Würdinger
AGENCY:
Gottschling & Würdinger
■ **281, 282**

PHOTOGRAPHER:
Hans Hansen
CLIENT:
Dibbern Collection
DESIGNER:
Randolph Nolte
■ **283**

■ **281, 282** "A design inspired by the forms of nature." Photo from a brochure offering a new line of silver cutlery marketed under the *Robbe & Berking* label. (GER)

■ **283** Photograph from the 1986 calendar from the "Dibbern Collection", a firm of wholesalers for household articles. (GER)

■ **281, 282** «Ein Design, inspiriert von den Formen der Natur.» Aufnahmen aus einem Prospekt für ein neues Silberbesteck der Marke *Robbe & Berking*. (GER)

■ **283** Aufnahme aus einem Kalender der «Dibbern Collection», eines Hamburger Grosshändlers für Haushaltartikel. (GER)

■ **281, 282** «Un design inspiré des formes de la nature.» Photos pour un dépliant présentant de nouveaux couverts d'argent *Robbe & Berking*. (GER)

■ **283** Photo pour un calendrier de la «Dibbern Collection» publié par un distributeur hambourgeois d'articles ménagers. (GER)

PHOTOGRAPHER:
Paul Franz-Moore

CLIENT:
Paul Franz-Moore

ART DIRECTOR:
Michael Osborne

DESIGNER:
Michael Osborne/
Bill Reuter

AGENCY:
Michael Osborne Design, Inc.

■ **284**

■ **284** Photo used as self promotion for the photographer Paul Franz-Moore of San Francisco. (USA)

■ **285** "Paris Bathroom, White on White." A personal study created by photographer Jay Maisel and included in the *"Mohawk Graphics Collection"* (paper producers). (USA)

■ **284** Als Eigenwerbung des Photographen Paul Franz-Moore, San Francisco, verwendete Aufnahme. (USA)

■ **285** »Pariser Badezimmer, Weiss auf Weiss.« Eine persönliche Studie des Photographen Jay Maisel, die in die »Graphik-Kollektion« des Papierherstellers *Mohawk* aufgenommen wurde. (USA)

■ **284** Photo utilisée pour sa promotion par le photographe Paul Franz-Moore de San Francisco. (USA)

■ **285** »Salle de bains parisienne, blanc sur blanc.« Etude personnelle du photographe Jay Maisel intégrée dans la »Collection graphique« du groupe papetier *Mohawk.* (USA)

PHOTOGRAPHER:
Jay Maisel

CLIENT:
*Mohawk
Paper Mills, Inc.*

ART DIRECTOR:
Jay Maisel

■285

PHOTOGRAPHER:
Peter Jones
CLIENT:
Polaroid
DESIGNER:
Paul Huber
■ **286**

PHOTOGRAPHER:
HARTWIG KLAPPERT
CLIENT:
HOSTMANN-STEINBERG
DRUCKFARBEN
■**287**

■**286** Photo from an advertising brochure: " *Polaroid:* Instant experience you can build on." (USA)

■**287** From a calendar for the German printing-ink producers *Hostmann-Steinberg* - a photo on the theme "Colors". (GER)

■**286** Aufnahme aus einer Werbebroschüre für *Polaroid:* «Unmittelbare Erfahrung, auf die Sie bauen können.» (USA)

■**287** Unter dem Aspekt «Farbe» verwendete Aufnahme aus einem Kalender für *Hostmann-Steinberg* Druckfarben. (GER)

■**286** Photo illustrant une brochure de *Polaroid:* «Une expérience instantanée sur laquelle vous pouvez compter.» (USA)

■**287** Photo sur le thème de la «couleur» utilisée dans un calendrier des encres d'imprimerie *Hostmann-Steinberg.* (GER)

◀◀ PP./S. 198/199

PHOTOGRAPHER:
BRUCE WOLF

CLIENT:
MARTEX/
WEST POINT PEPPERELL

ART DIRECTOR:
JAMES SEBASTIAN

DESIGNER:
JAMES SEBASTIAN/
JIM HINCHEE

STUDIO:
DESIGNFRAME INCORPORATED
■ 288

◀◀ Preceding spread:
■ **288** Double-spread photograph from a catalog for *Martex* home textiles. This shot serves as introduction to the following pages on which the flower-printed bedlinen collection by Sybil Connolly is presented. (USA)

◀◀ Vorangehende Doppelseite:
■ **288** Doppelseitige Aufnahme aus einem Katalog für *Martex*-Heimtextilien. Sie dient als Einleitung zu den nachfolgenden Seiten, auf denen eine Bettwäsche-Kollektion mit Blumenmotiven von Sybil Connolly vorgestellt wird. (USA)

◀◀ Double page précedente:
■ **288** Photo double page figurant dans un catalogue des tissus *Martex* pour la maison. Elle sert à introduire une section présentant une collection de linge de maison aux motifs fleuris créée par Sybil Connolly. (USA)

PHOTOGRAPHER:
Tom Vack/
Corinne Pfister

CLIENT:
City

ART DIRECTOR:
Robert Petrick

DESIGNER:
Robert Petrick

AGENCY:
Burson-Marsteller

■ **289-292**

■ **289-292** Full-page photographs from a catalog printed on synthetic paper in which the best designs of a store by the name of "City" are represented. *289* shows a cruet set by Achille Castiglioni (for the Officina Alessi Collection), *290* a coupe by Christian Duc, *291* a side chair by Robert Mallet-Stevens, and *292* side tables by Christian Duc. (USA)

■ **289-292** Aufnahmen aus einem auf synthetischem Papier gedruckten Katalog, in dem das beste Design eines Geschäftes mit dem Namen «City» vorgestellt wird. *289* zeigt Essig- und Ölkrüge von Achille Castiglioni, *290* eine Schale von Christian Duc, *291* einen Stuhl von Robert Mallet-Stevens, *292* Beisetztische von Christian Duc. (USA)

■ **289-292** Photos illustrant un catalogue produit sur papier synthétique où un magasin du nom de «City» présente le meilleur du design exposé. La photo *289* montre des huiliers proposés par l'artiste Achille Castiglioni, *290* une coupe de Christian Duc, *291* un siège de Robert Mallet-Stevens, *292* des tables gigognes créées par Christian Duc. (USA)

■ **293** Photograph of antique Japanese carpenter's tools used in the building of traditional-style wood-construction houses. From the book *Japan Design*. (JPN)

■ **294** Self-promotion photo for the photographer Bill White of New York. (USA)

■ **293** Aufnahme von antikem japanischem Zimmermannswerkzeug, das für den Bau der traditionellen Holzkonstruktionen der Häuser verwendet wurde. Aus dem Buch *Japan Design*. (JPN)

■ **294** Als Eigenwerbung verwendete Aufnahme des Photographen Bill White, New York. (USA)

■ **293** Photo d'outils traditionnels du charpentier japonais tels qu'on les employait pour construire les maisons en bois de l'archipel nippon. Extraite de l'ouvrage *Japan Design*. (JPN)

■ **294** Photo utilisée pour l'autopromotion du photographe newyorkais Bill White. (USA)

PHOTOGRAPHER:
HATAKEYAMA TAKASHI
PUBLISHER:
LIBRO PORT CO., LTD.
ART DIRECTOR:
IKKO TANAKA
DESIGNER:
KATSUHIRO KINOSHITA

■ **293**

PHOTOGRAPHER:
Bill White

CLIENT:
Bill White Studio

ART DIRECTOR:
Bill White

DESIGNER:
Peter Galperin

STUDIO:
Bill White Studio

■ 294

PHOTOGRAPHER:
Nob Fukuda
CLIENT:
Itokin Co., Ltd
ART DIRECTOR:
Tetsuro Sato
■ **295–298**

PHOTOGRAPHER:
Nob Fukuda
CLIENT:
Itokin Co., Ltd
ART DIRECTOR:
Tetsuro Sato

■ **295–298** "Fashion History 1920-1970" – photographs taken from a calendar. *295* relates to the thirties, *296* to the fifties, *297* to the twenties and *298* to the forties era. The photos within the photos: 1930s = Clarence Bull; 1950s = Richard Avedon; 1920s = Degy Hamilton; 1940 = John Miehle. (JPN)

■ **295–298** »Die Geschichte der Mode 1920–1970«, Aufnahmen aus einem Kalender. *295* bezieht sich auf die dreissiger, *296* auf die fünfziger, *297* auf die zwanziger und *298* auf die vierziger Jahre. Die Photos in den Aufnahmen: 1930 = Clarence Bull; 1950 = Richard Avedon; 1920 = Degy Hamilton; 1940s = John Miehle. (JPN)

■ **295–298** Ces photos illustrent un calendrier intitulé «Histoire de la mode 1920–1970». *295* évoque les années 1930, *296* les années 1950, *297* les années 1920 et *298* les années 1940. Les photos dans les photos: 1930 = Clarence Bull; 1950 = Richard Avedon; 1920 = Degy Hamilton; 1940 = John Miehle. (JPN)

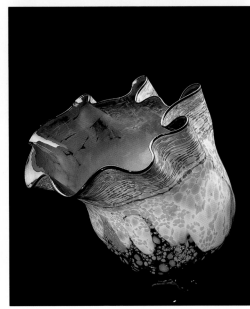

PHOTOGRAPHER:
Dick Busher

CLIENT:
Dick Busher Photography

ART DIRECTOR:
Jack Anderson

DESIGNER:
Jack Anderson/
Julie Tanagi

AGENCY:
Hornall Anderson
Design Works

■ 299-310

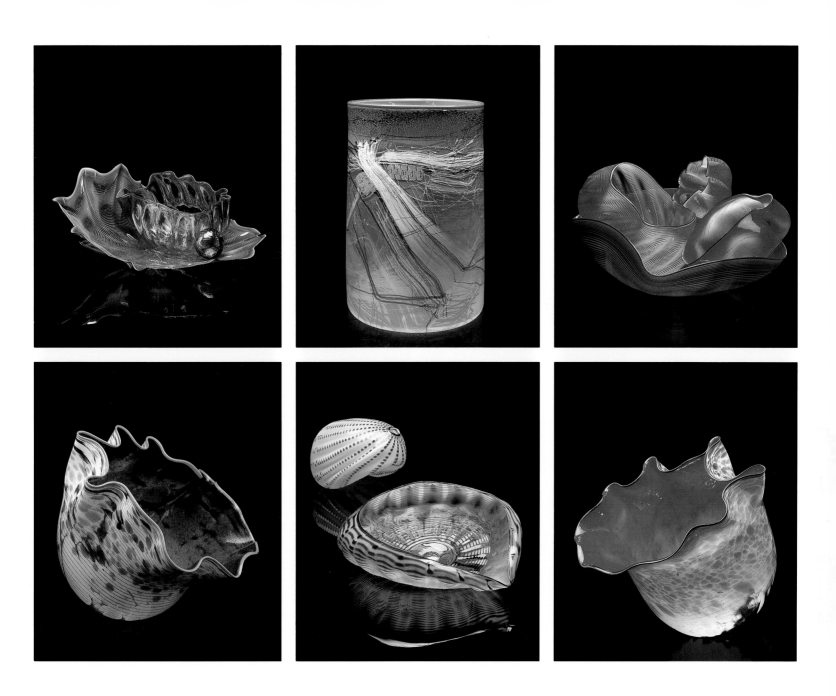

■ **299-310** Glass artist Dale Chihuly created the pieces shown in these photos. From a self-promotion calendar for Dick Busher; from Chihuly's "Sea Form sets" and his "Macchia" series. (USA)

■ **299-310** Glaskunst von Dale Chihuly ist Gegenstand dieser Aufnahmen aus einem Eigenwerbungskalender für Dick Busher. Die Themen sind «Formen des Meeres» und «Buntglas». (USA)

■ **299-310** Verrerie d'art de Dale Chihuly mise en photos pour un calendrier autopromotionnel de Dick Busher. Les séries montrées ici sont «Formes marines» et «Macchia». (USA)

■ **311-315** Photographs for a hanging calendar issued by American President Lines. Shown here are the letters of passport which give information about the ship and its crew (*311*); faces of Indians (papier maché) whose occupations, sects and stations of life are portrayed by the cut of beard and mustache, the cosmetic markings and the turbans (*312*); a Japanese Gosho Ningyo and a Kokeshi doll (*313*); coriander, cinnamon, coffee, and nutmeg from India (*314*) and the cover (*315*). (USA)

■ **311-315** Aufnahmen für einen Wandkalender der Reederei American President Lines. Hier die Schiffspapiere, die Auskunft über das Schiff und seine Besatzung geben (*311*); aus Papiermaché hergestellte Gesichter von indischen Männern verschiedener Stellung, die sich am Turban, Bart und an kosmetischen Zeichen ablesen lässt (*312*); eine japanische Gosho-Ningyo- und eine Kokeshi-Puppe, beide aus Holz (*313*); Koriander, Zimt, Kaffee und Muskatnuss aus Indien (*314*) und der Umschlag (*315*). (USA)

■ **311-315** Photos pour un calendrier mural de la compagnie de navigation American President Lines: papiers de bord renseignant sur le navire et l'équipage (*311*); visages d'indiens de différentes castes, en papier maché, reconnaissables à la barbe, au turban, aux signes de caste sur la peau (*312*); deux poupées japonaises en bois, la gosho-ningyo ou poupée du palais et la kokeshi (*313*); coriandre, cannelle, café, muscade indiens (*314*) et la couverture (*315*). (USA)

PHOTOGRAPHER:
Terry Heffernan

CLIENT:
American President Lines

ART DIRECTOR:
Kit Hinrichs

DESIGNER:
Kit Hinrichs/
Belle How

AGENCY:
Jonson Pedersen
Hinrichs & Shakery

■ 311-315

PHOTOGRAPHER:
JOE BARABAN

CLIENT:
SUPERB LITHO

DESIGNER:
JOHN WEAVER

AGENCY:
GLUTH/WEAVER

■ **318, 319**

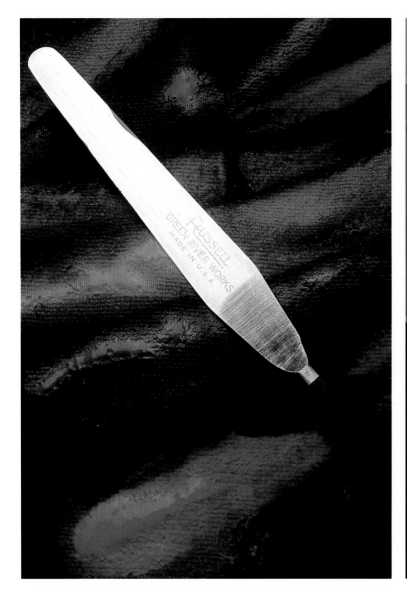 

■ **318, 319** Photographs from a diary issued by the lithographers Superb Litho Inc. to show their expertise. (USA)

■ **320** "First we'll get their attention..." - photograph for the cover of a brochure for *Caribiner*, a company who claims to be "the world's leading producer of quality meetings" (multimedia presentations). (USA)

■ **321** Photograph as self-promotional piece for the photographer Bill White of New York. (USA)

■ **318, 319** Aufnahmen aus einer Agenda, mit der die Lithographenfirma Superb Litho Inc. ihr Können unter Beweis stellt. (USA)

■ **320** «Zuerst erregen wir ihre Aufmerksamkeit...». Photo für den Umschlag eines Prospekts, mit dem ein Unternehmen Material und technische Anlagen für Konferenzen, Präsentationen, Vorträge usw. anbietet. (USA)

■ **321** Als Eigenwerbung verwendete Aufnahme des Photographen Bill White, New York. (USA)

■ **318, 319** Photos pour un agenda où l'atelier de litho Superb Litho Inc. démontre sa maîtrise du métier. (USA)

■ **320** «Tout d'abord, nous attirons leur attention...». Photo de couverture pour un dépliant où une entreprise propose du matériel et des installations techniques pour des séminaires, présentations, conférences, etc. (USA)

■ **321** Photo utilisée pour l'autopromotion du photographe Bill White de New York. (USA)

PHOTOGRAPHER:
Gavin Ashworth

CLIENT:
Caribiner

ART DIRECTOR:
Anthony Taibi

DESIGNER:
Constance Kovar

AGENCY:
Constance Kovar & Co.

■ 320

PHOTOGRAPHER:
Bill White

CLIENT:
Bill White Studio

DESIGNER:
Peter Galperin

■ 321

PHOTOGRAPHER:
Nikos Panayotopoulos
PUBLISHER:
Moressopulos & Assoc.
ART DIRECTOR:
Stavros Moressopulos
■324

■**325** Photo shot by Joe Baraban while on location for *Honda* Scooters ad campaign. (USA)

■**326** "Getting up Steam" is the caption of this photo used to illustrate the theme "Espresso" in *Playboy*. (GER)

■**325** Aufnahme, die als «Beiprodukt» von Werbeaufnahmen für *Honda*-Motorroller entstand. (USA)

■**326** Als Illustration zum Thema «Espresso» verwendete Aufnahme unter dem Motto «Macht mal Dampf», im *Playboy*. (GER)

■**325** Photo de Joe Baraban, prise lors des repérages pour la campagne de publicité des scooters *Honda*. (USA)

■**326** Photo sur le thème de l'«espresso» utilisée dans *Playboy* sous la devise «du nerf, les gars!» (GER)

PHOTOGRAPHER:
Ezio Geneletti
PUBLISHER:
Heinrich Bauer Verlag
ART DIRECTOR:
Manuel Ortiz
■326

PHOTOGRAPHER:
Joe Baraban
CLIENT:
Honda Scooters
ART DIRECTOR:
Susan Hoffman
AGENCY:
Wieden/Kennedy
■325

PHOTOGRAPHER:
Bernhard Angerer

CLIENT:
Hirsch

ART DIRECTOR:
F. Haubmann

DESIGNER:
F. Mätzler

AGENCY:
Demner & Merlicek

∎ 327, 328

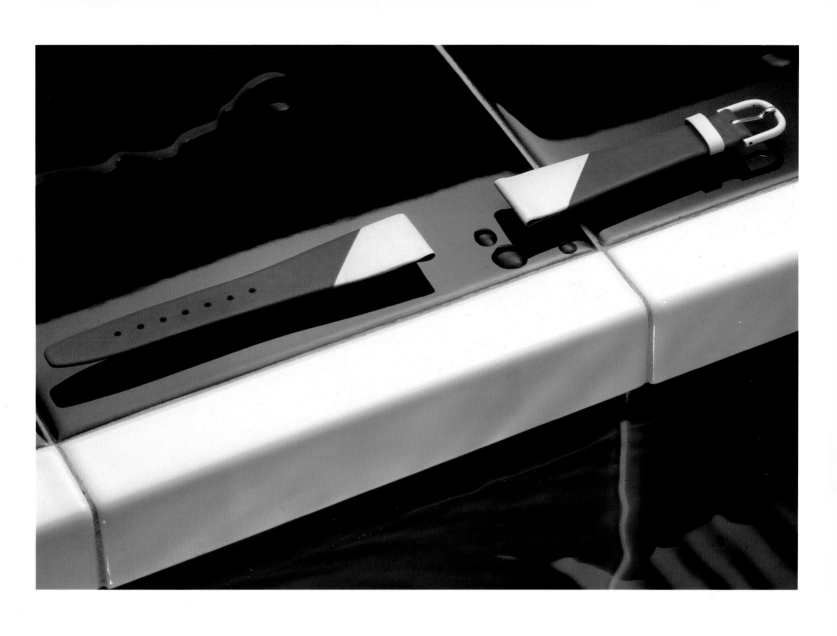

■ **327, 328** Double-spread ads from a catalog for watchstraps marketed under the *Hirsch* label. (AUT)

■ **327, 328** Doppelseitige Aufnahmen aus einem Katalog für Uhrenbänder der Marke *Hirsch*. (AUT)

■ **327, 328** Photos double page pour un catalogue des bracelets de montres de la marque *Hirsch*. (AUT)

■ **329, 330** Leather accessories are the subject of these photos which belong to a series appearing in *Vogue Paris*. *329* shows articles from various well-known designers, *330* shopping bags by *Louis Vuitton* – "shopping chic." (FRA)

■ **331, 332** The setting is the Park Hotel, Siena, for these photos from an ad campaign for cases by MCM of München. (GER)

■ **329, 330** Leder-Accessoires sind Gegenstand dieser Aufnahmen, die zu einer in *Vogue Paris* erschienenen Serie gehören. *329* zeigt Artikel von verschiedenen bekannten Designern, *330* Einkaufstaschen von *Louis Vuitton*. (FRA)

■ **331, 332** Im Park-Hotel, Siena, entstandene Aufnahmen aus einer Werbekampagne für Koffer von MCM, München. (GER)

■ **329, 330** Ces photos d'accessoires en cuir illustrent une série parue dans *Vogue Paris*. La fig. *329* réunit des articles dus à divers designers réputés; la fig. *330* présente les sacs *Louis Vuitton* pour le shopping chic. (FRA)

■ **331, 332** Photos réalisées au Parc-Hôtel de Sienne pour une campagne en faveur des valises MCM (Munich). (GER)

Courtesy Vogue, Paris - Copyright © 1986 by Les Editions Condé Nast S. A.

Courtesy Vogue, Paris - Copyright © 1986 by Les Editions Condé Nast S. A.

PHOTOGRAPHER:
Oliver Mauffrey/
Louis Gaillard
PUBLISHER:
Condé Nast S.A.
ART DIRECTOR:
Paul Wagner
■ **329, 330**

PHOTOGRAPHER:
Dietmar Henneka

CLIENT:
MCM München

ART DIRECTOR:
Urs Schwerzmann

AGENCY:
Büro Schwerzmann

■ 331, 332

PHOTOGRAPHER:
Terry Heffernan

CLIENT:
National Press

ART DIRECTOR:
Steven Tolleson

DESIGNER:
Steven Tolleson/
Susan Gross

AGENCY:
Tolleson Design

■ **333-335**

PHOTOGRAPHER:
Victor Budnik
CLIENT:
Paige Johnson Design, Inc.
ART DIRECTOR:
Paige Johnson Roetter
DESIGNER:
Paige Johnson Roetter
AGENCY:
Paige Johnson Design, Inc.
■ 336

■ **336** Photograph from a self-promotion brochure for Paige Johnson Design. Shown is one manner of presenting fashion (for example by *Ralph Lauren*) which is meant to portray a particularly traditional lifestyle. (USA)

■ **337, 338** Photos from a double-spread ad for shoes by *Nina*: "eeeeeeendlessss color from heel to toe." (USA)

■ **336** Aufnahme aus einer Eigenwerbungsbroschüre für Paige Johnson Design. Hier eine Darstellungsmöglichkeit für Mode (z.B. von *Ralph Lauren*), die ein bestimmtes, traditionsverbundenes Lebensgefühl vermitteln soll. (USA)

■ **337, 338** Aufnahmen aus einem doppelseitigen Inserat für *Nina*-Schuhe: «Unendliche Farbe von Hacke bis Spitze.» (USA)

■ **336** Photo d'une brochure autopromotionnelle pour Paige Johnson Design. Ici, une façon de présenter la mode (de *Ralph Lauren*, par ex.) qui tend à communiquer un certain sentiment de la vie, rattaché aux traditions. (USA)

■ **337, 338** Photos pour une annonce double page pour les chaussures *Nina*: «couleur infinie du talon jusqu'au bout.» (USA)

PHOTOGRAPHER:
Ben Rosenthal
CLIENT:
Nina Footwear
ART DIRECTOR:
Beth Schack
DESIGNER:
Beth Schack
AGENCY:
Don Wise & Co.
■ **337, 338**

PHOTOGRAPHER:
Michel Perez

CLIENT:
Boutique L'Uomo

ART DIRECTOR:
Ikram Schelhot

DESIGNER:
Ikram Schelhot

AGENCY:
Concept I. S.

■ **339-342**

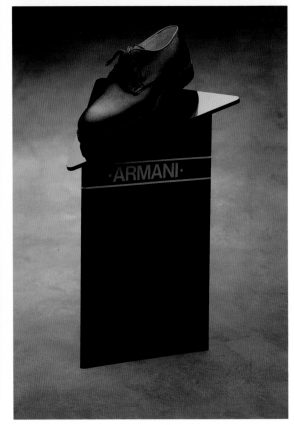

■ **339-342** Photos from a catalog for the boutique L'Uomo in Montréal. (CAN)

■ **343** Photo from an ad for shoes marketed under the *Casadei* label, appearing in *Vogue Italia*. (ITA)

■ **339-342** Aufnahmen aus einem Katalog für die Boutique L'Uomo in Montréal. (CAN)

■ **343** Aufnahme aus einem Inserat für Schuhe der Marke *Casadei*, erschienen in *Vogue Italia*. (ITA)

■ **339-342** Photos pour un catalogue de la boutique L'Uomo à Montréal. (CAN)

■ **343** Photo illustrant une annonce parue dans *Vogue Italia*: chaussures de la marque *Casadei*. (ITA)

PHOTOGRAPHER:
Piero Gemelli

CLIENT:
Casadei

ART DIRECTOR:
Piero Gemelli

DESIGNER:
Piero Gemelli

STUDIO:
Barbara Falanga

■ **343**

■**344** Photo from a series of advertisements for industrial design, created by an international group of designers, who work under the name of *frogdesign*. (GER)

■**344** Aus einer Serie von Anzeigen für Industrie-Design, geschaffen von einer internationalen Gruppe von Designern, die unter der Bezeichnung *frogdesign* zusammenarbeiten. (GER)

■**344** Photo illustrant l'une des annonces réalisées pour les créations d'esthétique industrielle d'un groupe international de designers travaillant sous le nom de *frogdesign*. (GER)

PHOTOGRAPHER:
VICTOR GOICO
CLIENT:
FROGDESIGN
ART DIRECTOR:
VICTOR GOICO
STUDIO:
VICTOR GOICO
■**344**

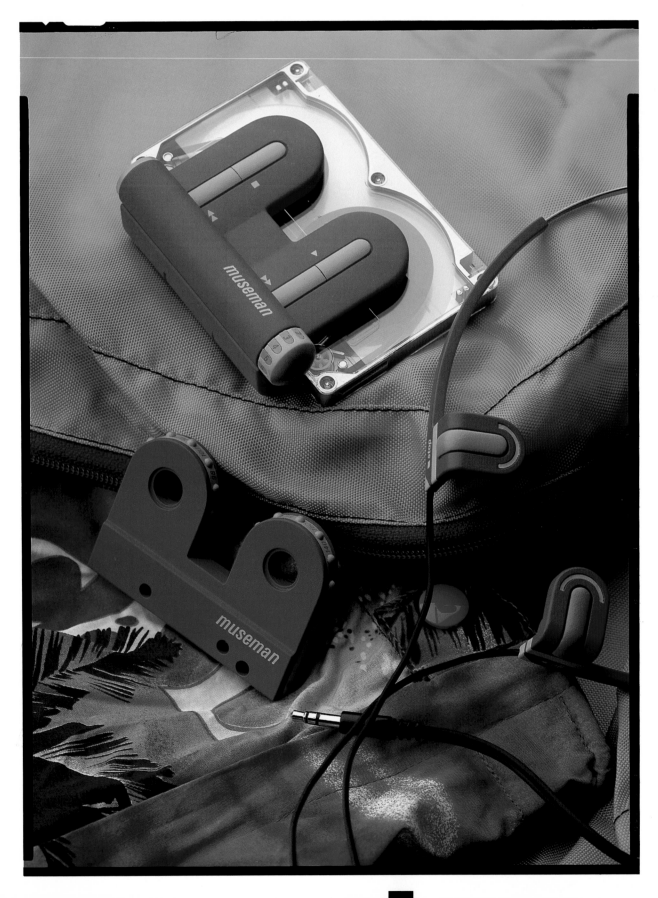

PHOTOGRAPHER:
François Gillet
CLIENT:
St-Andros
ART DIRECTOR:
Michael Partridge/
Nathalie Lebarazer
AGENCY:
Futurs
■ 345

■**345** Full-page photograph for *Bonne Maman* jams – "Pure Fruit, Pure Tenderness." (FRA)

■**346, 347** Photographs in black and white from a series of double-page advertisements for "Les Vins de Pays, Wines from the Homely Provinces of France." (GER)

■**345** Ganzseitige Aufnahme für Konfitüre der Marke *Bonne Maman:* »Reine Frucht, reine Zärtlichkeit.« (FRA)

■**346, 347** Aufnahmen in Schwarzweiss aus einer Serie von doppelseitigen Inseraten für »Les Vins de Pays, Weine aus den ländlichen Provinzen Frankreichs«. (GER)

■**345** Photo pleine page pour les confitures de la marque *Bonne Maman:* »Pur fruit, pure tendresse«. (FRA)

■**346, 347** Photos noir et blanc d'une série d'annonces sur double page pour »Les Vins de Pays«, des vins du terroir provenant de diverses provinces de la France. (GER)

PHOTOGRAPHER:
Christian Délu

CLIENT:
Sopexa

ART DIRECTOR:
Klaus Heckhoff/
Hermann Gottschalk

DESIGNER:
B. Merten

AGENCY:
IdeenService

■ **346, 347**

PHOTOGRAPHER:
Carol Kaplan

CLIENT:
Kaplan Studio, Inc.

ART DIRECTOR:
Vic Cevoli

DESIGNER:
Jeff Katz

STUDIO:
Kaplan Studio, Inc.

■ 348

■ **348** "Bowls." Photograph as self-promotional piece by photographer Carol Kaplan of Boston. (USA)

■ **349** "Continental Breakfast." Photograph for a self-promotion poster for Yuri Dojc, a photographer living in Toronto. (CAN)

■ **348** -Schalen.- Als Eigenwerbung verwendete Aufnahme der Photographin Carol Kaplan, Boston. (USA)

■ **349** -Kleines Frühstück.- Aufnahme für ein Eigenwerbungsplakat des Photographen Yuri Dojc, Toronto. (CAN)

■ **348** «Bols.» Photo utilisée pour l'autopromotion de la photographe Carol Kaplan de Boston. (USA)

■ **349** «Petit déjeuner.» Photo pour une affiche autopromotionnelle du photographe Yuri Dojc de Toronto. (CAN)

PHOTOGRAPHER:
Yuri Dojc

CLIENT:
Yuri Dojc Inc.

DESIGNER:
Taylor & Browning Design

STUDIO:
Yuri Dojc Inc.

■ **349**

PHOTOGRAPHER:
Kathryn Kleinman

PUBLISHER:
Chronicle Books

ART DIRECTOR:
Kathryn Kleinman/
Amy Nathan

DESIGNER:
Jacqueline Jones
■ 350–354

■**350—354** Photographs from the book *Salad* by Amy Nathan, published by *Chronicle Books*, San Francisco. *350* shows a summer salad from three varieties of tomatoes, *351* a winter salad with toasted walnuts; *352* shows the cover photograph, *353* introduces a chapter about diverse oils and vinegars, *354* is an array that evokes the beauty of a walk in the woods. (USA)

■**350—354** Aufnahmen für ein bei *Chronicle Books*, San Francisco, erschienenes Buch von Amy Nathan über Salat. *350* zeigt einen Sommersalat aus drei Sorten Tomaten, *351* einen Wintersalat mit gerösteten Walnüssen, *352* zeigt die Umschlagaufnahme, *353* leitet ein Kapitel über Öl- und Essigsorten ein, *354* ist ein Arrangement, das an einen Waldspaziergang erinnert. (USA)

■**350—354** Photos d'un livre d'Amy Nathan sur la salade, paru chez *Chronicle Books*, San Francisco. La photo *350* montre une salade estivale faite de trois sortes de tomates, *351* une salade d'hiver aux noix grillées, *352* est la photo de couverture, *353* en tête d'un chapitre sur les huiles et les vinaigres divers, *354* une préparation qui évoque une promenade dans les bois. (USA)

PHOTOGRAPHER:
Christian von Alvensleben
PUBLISHER:
Condé Nast Verlag GmbH
ART DIRECTOR:
Angelica Blechschmidt
■ 355–358

■ **355–358** Full-page photographs from the recipe section of the German edition of *Vogue. 355* game; *356* shell-fish; *357* Japanese cookery; *358* carp dish for Christmas and New Year. (GER)

■ **355–358** Ganzseitige Aufnahmen aus dem Rezeptteil der deutschen *Vogue. 355* Wildgericht; *356* Muschelgericht; *357* japanische Küche; *358* Karpfengerichte für die Festtage. (GER)

■ **355–358** Photos pleine page de la rubrique «Cuisine» du *Vogue* allemand. *355* gibier; *356* moules; *357* recettes de cuisine japonaise; *358* recettes de carpes pour les fêtes. (GER)

ZEITSCHRIFT	WELT:	BRD:
☐ **GRAPHIS** (1 Jahr/6 Ausgaben)	SFr. 118.—	DM 146,—
☐ **1986er PORTFOLIO**-Schachtel (n) (für 6 Hefte)	SFr. 19.—	DM 24,—

Jahresabonnement Schweiz Fr. 114.—. Porto, Verpackung und Bearbeitungsgebühren sind im Abonnements-Preis inbegriffen, ausser der Einschreibegebühr von SFr. 12.— für Lateinamerika und Indien.

☐ Studierende erhalten eine Ermässigung von 25%. Bitte eine Ausweiskopie beilegen.

BÜCHER	CH/WELT:	BRD:
☐ GRAPHIS POSTERS 87	SFr. 105.—	DM 129,—
☐ GRAPHIS ANNUAL 86/87	SFr. 112.—	DM 138,—
☐ PHOTOGRAPHIS 86	SFr. 112.—	DM 138,—
☐ GRAPHIS POSTERS 86	SFr. 105.—	DM 129,—
☐ ARCHIGRAPHIA	SFr. 74.—	DM 92,—
☐ FILM + TV GRAPHICS 2	SFr. 69.—	DM 86,—
☐ KINDERBUCH-ILLUSTRATION 4	SFr. 45.—	DM 56,—
☐ 65TH NEW YORK ADA *	SFr. 96.—*	DM 118,—
☐ GRAPHIC DESIGN USA: 7*	SFr. 96.—*	DM 118,—
☐ TYPOGRAPHY 7*	SFr. 68.—*	DM 84,00
☐ ADLA: 2*	SFr. 79.—*	DM 98,—
☐ ILLUSTRATORS 27*	SFr. 110.—*	DM 135,—
☐ CHWAST: LEFT HANDED DESIGNER*	SFr. 74.—*	DM 89,—

Die mit einem Stern (*) bezeichneten Titel können nur in europäische Länder geliefert werden.

☐ Scheck liegt bei (SFr.-Schecks bitte auf eine Schweizer Bank ziehen)
☐ Betrag überwiesen auf Ihr Konto bei der Schweizerischen Bankgesellschaft, 8021 Zürich
☐ Betrag überwiesen auf PC Zürich 80-23071-9/PSchK Frankfurt a.M. 3000 57-602
☐ Bitte stellen Sie Rechnung (Versandspesen zusätzlich zu obigen Bücher-Preisen)

NAME

BERUF

ADRESSE

DATUM **UNTERSCHRIFT**

GRAPHIS VERLAG AG, DUFOURSTRASSE 107, CH-8008 ZÜRICH (SCHWEIZ)

MAGAZINE	WORLD:	USA:	CAN.:	U.K.:
☐ **GRAPHIS** (one year/6 issues)	SFr. 118.—	$59.00	$82.00	£45.00
☐ **1986 PORTFOLIO** (case holds 6 issues)	SFr. 19.—	$11.00	$15.00	£ 8.00

Postage, carton and handling fees are included in the above subscription rates with the exception of the registering fee of SFr. 12.— for Latin American countries and India.

☐ Students may request a 25% reduction by sending student identification.

BOOKS	WORLD:	USA:	U.K.:
☐ GRAPHIS POSTERS 87	SFr.105.—	US$59.50*	£42.00
☐ GRAPHIS ANNUAL 86/87	SFr.112.—	US$59.50*	£45.00
☐ PHOTOGRAPHIS 86	SFr.112.—	US$59.50*	£45.00
☐ GRAPHIS POSTERS 86	SFr.105.—	US$59.50*	£42.00
☐ ARCHIGRAPHIA	SFr. 74.—	US$42.50	£29.00
☐ FILM + TV GRAPHICS 2	SFr. 69.—	US$39.50	£27.00
☐ CHILDREN'S BOOK ILL. 4	SFr. 45.—	US$24.00	£18.00
☐ 65TH NEW YORK ADA **	SFr. 96.—	**	£39.00
☐ GRAPHIC DESIGN USA: 7**	SFr. 96.—	**	£39.00
☐ TYPOGRAPHY 7**	SFr. 68.—	**	£28.00
☐ ADLA: 2**	SFr. 79.—	**	£32.00
☐ ILLUSTRATORS 27**	SFr.110.—	**	£43.00
☐ CHWAST: LEFT HANDED DES.**	SFr. 74.—	**	£29.00

Please note that the above asterisks mean the following:
*Send orders to: Watson Guptill Publications, P.O.B. 2014, Lakewood, N.J. 08701
**For delivery only in Europe including Great Britain.

☐ Check enclosed (For Europe, please make SFr.-checks payable to a Swiss bank)
☐ Amount paid into your account at the Swiss Bank Corp. in New York, London or Zurich.
☐ Amount paid to Postal Cheque Account Zurich 80-23071-9 (through your local postoffice)
☐ Send invoice (mailing costs in addition to above book prices)

NAME

PROFESSION

ADDRESS

DATE **SIGNATURE**

For U.S. and Canada:
GRAPHIS U.S. INC., 141 LEXINGTON AVENUE, NEW YORK, NY 10016, U.S.A.
For Europe, please send to:
GRAPHIS PRESS CORP., DUFOURSTRASSE 107, CH-8008 ZÜRICH (SWITZERLAND)

REVUE	TOUT PAYS:	FRANCE:
☐ **GRAPHIS** (abonnement annuel/6 numéros)	FS 118.—	FF 495.00
☐ **PORTFOLIO 1986** (boîte pour 6 numéros)	FS 19.—	FF 95.00

Prix d'abonnement pour la Suisse Fr. 114.—. Le port, l'emballage et les frais sont compris dans le prix d'abonnement, sauf les frais de port recommandé pour l'Amérique Latine et l'Inde.

☐ Réduction de 25% pour les étudiants. Prière de joindre une photocopie de la carte d'étudiant.

LIVRES	SUI/TOUT PAYS:	FRANCE:
☐ GRAPHIS POSTERS 87	FS 105.—	FF 445.00
☐ GRAPHIS ANNUAL 86/87	FS 112.—	FF 475.00
☐ PHOTOGRAPHIS 86	FS 112.—	FF 475.00
☐ GRAPHIS POSTERS 86	FS 105.—	FF 445.00
☐ ARCHIGRAPHIA	FS 74.—	FF 315.00
☐ FILM + TV GRAPHICS 2	FS 69.—	FF 295.00
☐ ILLUSTR. DE LIVRES D'ENFANTS 4	FS 45.—	FF 195.00
☐ 65TH NEW YORK ADA*	FS 96.—*	FF 410.00
☐ GRAPHIC DESIGN USA: 7*	FS 96.—*	FF 410.00
☐ TYPOGRAPHY 7*	FS 68.—*	FF 290.00
☐ ADLA: 2*	FS 79.—*	FF 340.00
☐ ILLUSTRATORS 27*	FS 110.—*	FF 465.00
☐ CHWAST: LEFT HANDED DESIGNER*	FS 74.—*	FF 315.00

*Livraison en Europe seulement.

☐ Chèque bancaire ci-joint (prière de tirer les chèques en FS sur une banque Suisse)
☐ Règlement adressé à votre compte auprès de l'UBS, 8021 Zurich
☐ Règlement adressé au CCP Editions Graphis, Zurich 80-23071-9
☐ Facture demandée (frais de transport en sus du prix des livres indiqué ci-dessus)

NOM

PROFESSION

ADRESSE

DATE **SIGNATURE**

EDITIONS GRAPHIS SA, DUFOURSTRASSE 107, CH-8008 ZURICH (SUISSE)

REQUEST FOR CALL FOR ENTRIES

BITTE UM EINSENDEBEDINGUNGEN
RECOMMANDATIONS POUR L'ENVOI

■ Please put me on your "Call for Entries" list for the following annuals (check the appropriate box or boxes)*

■ Bitte setzen Sie meinen Namen auf Ihre "Einladungs"-Liste für die folgenden Jahrbücher (bitte die entsprechenden Felder ankreuzen)*

■ Veuillez inscrire mon nom sur la liste d'invitation des prochains annuels (mettre une croix dans la case correspondante)*

☐ **GRAPHIS ANNUAL**   ☐ **PHOTOGRAPHIS**   ☐ **GRAPHIS POSTERS**
☐ **PACKAGING**   ☐ **DIAGRAMS**   ☐ **ANNUAL REPORTS**

*By submitting material to any of the above annuals, you will qualify for a 25% discount towards purchase of that annual.

*Durch Ihre Einsendung für eines der oben erwähnten Jahrbücher erhalten Sie 25% Rabatt auf den Verkaufspreis des betreffenden Buches.

*Pour chaque envoi concernant l'un des annuels de cette liste, vous bénéficierez de 25% de réduction sur le prix du livre.

NAME/NOM

PROFESSION/BERUF

STREET/STRASSE/RUE

CITY/ORT/LIEU **ZIP/PLZ/CEDEX**

COUNTRY/LAND/PAYS

LANGUAGE CHOICE/WAHL DER SPRACHVERSION/CHOIX DE LA LANGUE

If you have received the NEW *Graphis* in a language other than your preference, please mark your choice and return the card.

☐ **GERMAN** ☐ **FRENCH** ☐ **ENGLISH**

In the future, we may consider other language versions. Please give us your suggestion:

PLEASE SEND ORDER FORM IN SEALED ENVELOPE TO:

GRAPHIS PRESS. CORP.
107 DUFOURSTRASSE
CH-8008 ZURICH/SWITZERLAND

IN USA (FOR BOOKS MARKED WITH * ONLY):

WATSON-GUPTILL PUBLICATIONS
P.O. BOX 2014
LAKEWOOD, N.J. 08701

BESTELLKARTE BITTE IN VERSCHLOSSENEM UMSCHLAG EINSENDEN AN:

GRAPHIS VERLAG AG
DUFOURSTRASSE 107
CH-8008 ZÜRICH

BESTELLKARTE BITTE IN VERSCHLOSSENEM UMSCHLAG EINSENDEN AN:

GRAPHIS VERLAG AG
DUFOURSTRASSE 107
CH-8008 ZÜRICH

GRAPHIS U.S. INC.
141 LEXINGTON AVENUE
NEW YORK, N.Y. 10016

VEUILLEZ ADRESSER LE BON DE COMMANDE DANS UNE ENVELOPPE FERMÉE AUX:

EDITIONS GRAPHIS SA
107, DUFOURSTRASSE
CH-8008 ZURICH/SUISSE